The World at Peace and

1890–1930

Roy Wilsher

Oliver & Boyd

Acknowledgements

The author and publishers are grateful to the following for permission to reproduce photographic material:

Central Bibliothek, Zurich: page 16; The Daily Mirror Archives: page 37 (left); Dean and Chapter of Westminster: 54 (left); Hulton-Deutsch Collection: pages 19 (left), 41 (left), 44 (top), 54 (2 right), 64; Imperial War Museum: pages 13, 26 (left), 27, 28 (2), 29 (3), 30 (2), 31, 32, 39, 40 (3), 43 (right & left), 46, 50, 51, 52; The Mansell Collection: page 18 (2): Mary Evans: page 43 (centre); Popperfoto: page 77; Punch: pages 12 (right), 17, 19 (right), 21, 24, 42, 47, 62, 65 (top), 70, 73, 74 (left); Purnell's History of the Second World War: pages 6, 9 (bottom), 14, 15, 55 (2), 66 (top), 68; Roger-Viollet: page 12 (left); Facsimilequerschnitt durch den Simplicissimus: page 74 (right); Snark: page 9 (top); Topham Picture Library: pages 41 (right), 44 (bottom), 49; Weimar Archive: page 10; By courtesy of the Dean and Chapter of Westminster, page 54 (left).

We are unable to trace the copyright holders of the following and would be grateful for any information that would enable us to do so: pages 26 (right), 37 (centre), 37 (right), 43 (bottom right), 45, 48, 57, 65 (bottom), 69, 75, 76.

The authors and publishers are also grateful to The Imperial War Museum for permission to reproduce extracts from *With a Machine Gun Cambrai* by George Coppard.

Designed and illustrated by Cauldron Design Studio, Berwickshire.

Oliver & Boyd
Longman House
Burnt Mill
Harlow, Essex,
CM20 2JE, England

An Imprint of Longman Group UK Ltd and Associated Companies throughout the world

ISBN 0 05 004486 9
First published 1991
Third impression 1992

Typeset on an Apple Macintosh SE/30

Produced by Longman Singapore Publishers (Pte) Ltd
Printed in Singapore

Contents

Foreword

Written for use as a basic textbook for Foundation/General courses in the Standard Grade of the Scottish Examination Board, the aim has been to provide a simple story-line which will activate pupils' interest. All the key ideas and concepts for Unit II Context B of the syllabus are covered. The core content is geared to Foundation Level and the Extensions to General Level. The work section in each Unit and the Assignments in the Extensions are based upon the Grade Related Criteria for the syllabus.

Opportunities are given for inter-active learning and for debate throughout the book and the table on p. 5 shows the principal topics, concepts and key ideas.

I gratefully acknowledge assistance from Phil Gaskell of Castlebrae High School, Edinburgh, who has given invaluable advice on the readability of the text.

Roy Wilsher
March 1991

Synopsis for Teachers

Unit	Content	Key Idea	Concept
1	**Nations in 1890:** Meaning of nation and nationalism. Nations and people. Great powers and their relative positions in world. German–British rivalry. Franco–German rivalry. Austro–Hungarian–Russian rivalry. The Kaiser's ambitions. Naval competition.	Attitudes and actions of nations had international repercussions	Nation Inter-dependence Power Influence
2	**The Road to War:** Defensive alliances (Triple Alliance, Dual Entente, Entente Cordiale, Triple Entente) – the 'Armed Camps'. Moroccan Crises 1905–11 – repercussions. Balkan Crises 1908–13. Sarajevo – repercussions. Outbreak of war, 1914.	Attitudes and actions of nations had international repercussions	Nation Inter-dependence
3	**Men and Machines of War:** Start of the War – invasion of Belgium. Schlieffen Plan and its failure. Trench warfare – new technology and its effects. Recruiting Campaign. Life in the trenches. Battle of the Somme as example of attempted breakthrough.	People's lives were affected by international tension and war	Conflict
4	**The Home Fronts:** Experience of war at home in Britain: DORA, censorship, propaganda, labour relations (Red Clydeside), women at work, enemy aliens, food supplies and rationing, Zeppelin raids. Effect of war on Germany – economic blockade and impact on German life.	People's lives were affected by international tension and war	Conflict
5	**The End of the War:** Attitude of U.S.A. to war. Impact of American entry. German Spring Offensive and final defeat. Effects of the War – casualties, cost in money and destruction. Aims of the victors – Wilson and the 14 points. Treaty of Versailles – terms, effects. German reaction to Treaty. Emergence of U.S.A. as world leader. Britain's decline in influence. Impact of peace on people in Germany and Britain.	Status and influence of countries changed as circumstances changed. People's lives were affected by the restoration of peace	Peace Power Influence Nation
6	**The League of Nations:** Impact of President Wilson and his views. Attitudes of American, French, and British to League. Aims, organisation and methods of League. Membership of the League. Successes and failures of League. League's weakness.	Experience of war and its consequences affected attitudes towards peace and disarmament	Security Peace
7	**International Co-Operation:** Nations in 1920. German and French attitudes to reparations. Occupation of the Ruhr. Stresemann and German foreign policy. Problem of security. Treaty of Locarno. Kellogg–Briand Pact. Movement for disarmament. Treaty of Washington.	Experience of war and its consequences affected attitudes towards peace and disarmament	Security Disarmament Peace

1 Nations in 1890

Source 1.1

A **B** **C**

Nations and People

Nations often behave like ordinary people. Nations and ordinary people can both have friends and enemies. They can live together peacefully. They can quarrel. They can even fight!

Nations can be so like ordinary people that in *cartoons* the artist often uses a person to stand for a nation. Britain is sometimes shown as 'John Bull', France as 'Marianne' and the United States of America as 'Uncle Sam'.

When we talk about nations we say 'her' and 'she', even if the nation is shown as a male figure in cartoons.

> ### WHAT YOU WILL LEARN
>
> Unit 1 will help you to understand:
>
> 1 What a nation is.
> 2 That some nations are more powerful than others.
> 3 That nations often behave like ordinary people.
> 4 That nations depend upon each other.
> 5 How nations were related to each other in the 1890s.

▓▓ WORK SECTION ▓▓

Look at the figures in source 1.1 taken from cartoons. Answer these questions:
1 Which nations do A, B and C stand for?
2 What sort of person is 'John Bull'? Is he skinny, proud, angry or poor?

The Power of Nations

In the next source you can look at the most powerful nations in the years between 1890 and 1900. Notice that all the most powerful nations, except two, were in Europe. This made Europe the strongest continent in the world at that time.

Notice that these most powerful nations didn't all have the same amount of *power*. Some were more powerful than others.

The most powerful of all the powerful nations were sometimes called the Great Powers. They could *influence* weak nations and make them obey.

Source 1.2

This shows the size of the Great Powers and their *empires* in square miles

Power	Home territory	Overseas empire
Great Britain	120 979	10 500 000
Russia	8 660 395	–
France	204 092	4 367 000
U.S.A.	2 939 000	620 000
Germany	208 830	1 000 000
Austria-Hungary	264 204	–
Italy	110 646	185 000
Japan	147 655	14 000

(From Purnell's *History of the Twentieth Century*)

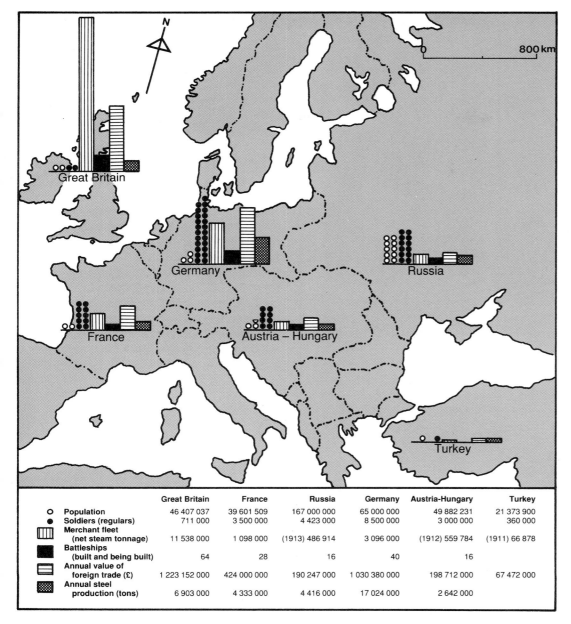

		Great Britain	France	Russia	Germany	Austria-Hungary	Turkey
○	**Population**	46 407 037	39 601 509	167 000 000	65 000 000	49 882 231	21 373 900
●	**Soldiers (regulars)**	711 000	3 500 000	4 423 000	8 500 000	3 000 000	360 000
▥	**Merchant fleet (net steam tonnage)**	11 538 000	1 098 000	(1913) 486 914	3 096 000	(1912) 559 784	(1911) 66 878
■	**Battleships (built and being built)**	64	28	16	40	16	
▤	**Annual value of foreign trade (£)**	1 223 152 000	424 000 000	190 247 000	1 030 380 000	198 712 000	67 472 000
▦	**Annual steel production (tons)**	6 903 000	4 333 000	4 416 000	17 024 000	2 642 000	

WORK SECTION

1 Which two non-European nations claimed to be Great Powers in the 1890s?
2 Which Great Power had the greatest population and which had the largest regular army?
3 Which nation had the biggest overseas empire?
4 Write down two other reasons why Britain could claim to be the most powerful nation of all.
5 Make a simple bar chart to compare the size of the overseas empires belonging to the Great Powers.

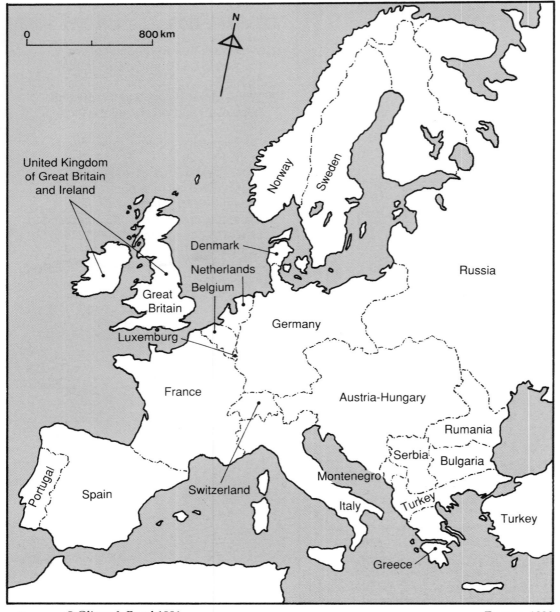

Europe, 1890

The Great Powers of Europe

On the left is a map of Europe in 1890

Italy had not been a united nation for very long. She wanted to have a great empire but the older nations had not left much room in the world. Italy did manage to take over a few unwanted bits of Africa and then, in 1896, Italy invaded Abyssinia (now called Ethiopia). But the Abyssinians defeated the Italian army. Abyssinia stayed independent under its own black ruler. Italy felt disappointed and hurt by her defeat.

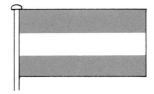

Austria-Hungary was proud of her Empire. It covered a great chunk of central Europe and did not include any territory overseas. Her ruler was the Emperor Francis Joseph II. He ruled over many different nations speaking many different languages. These nations wanted to become *independent*.

© Oliver & Boyd 1991

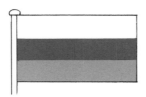

Russia also had an empire on her doorstep without any lands overseas. The huge size of the Russian Empire made her look strong. But she was not as strong as she looked. Most of her people were uneducated and poor. Russia was behind the other Great Powers in improving her factories and mines. Her ruler was the Emperor (or Tsar) Nicholas II.

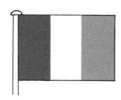

France had always been a proud and important nation in Europe. But in 1870 she was defeated by the biggest German state, Prussia. Prussia then took away Alsace-Lorraine from France. French pride was hurt. She wanted to take revenge against Germany and win back Alsace-Lorraine.

The French Empire was mainly in Africa. It was smaller than the British Empire but much larger than the German Empire.

France was a nation ruled by a president instead of a king or emperor. Such nations are called republics.

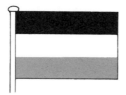

Germany had not been a united nation for very long. Now her ruler, the Emperor (or Kaiser) William II, wanted to make his nation the greatest and most important in the world. Most of all he wanted to gain a bigger empire for Germany. Before 1890 Germany had got hold of four areas of land in Africa but these needed developing. The Kaiser also wanted to build up a bigger navy and strengthen his army.

Great Britain had the largest, richest and most powerful Empire in the world in 1890. It was protected by the world's largest and strongest navy. The Empire and the navy made Britain the greatest of all the Great Powers of Europe. Queen Victoria and her Prime Minister hoped to keep it that way!

WORK SECTION

1 Look at source 1.3.
   a) Who is at the centre of the stamp and the cartoon?

Source 1.3

Two views of the Kaiser William II. A German 5-mark stamp and a British cartoon of 1914

   b) The words 'Deutsches Reich' mean German Empire. Try to translate into English the other German words.
   c) When Germans saw the stamp what would they think about their nation and her leader?
   d) What would British people think about the German Emperor when they saw the cartoon?
2 Why did France want to take revenge on Germany?

3 Why did Italy fail to gain a bigger empire at that time?

4 Copy this note and fill in the gaps:
The British Empire needed a strong navy because the Empire was overseas and not close to _____. British lands were in many parts of the _____. Also British lands had to be _____ from enemies.

Powers in 1890 using a different colour for each. Find out the names of their capital cities and put each one in its correct place on your map. Use an atlas to help you.

WORK SECTION

Look at source 1.5.
1 Draw a bar chart to show clearly a comparison between the German and British build-up of dreadnoughts from 1906 to 1914.

2 Did Britain or Germany win the naval race? Look back at source 1.2.
3 Did Britain or Germany have the bigger army?
4 Which was more important for Britain's defence, the army or the navy? Give a reason for your answer.

Rivalry between the Nations

The nations which were Great Powers often tried to boss about the small independent nations. This meant the small nations had to depend on each other, helping each other stand up to the Great Powers.

The Great Powers didn't depend on each other. Instead they were rivals, competing against each other. Each wanted a bigger empire, more trade, and a stronger army and navy than other nations had. They didn't trust each other.

When people are rivals, it sometimes ends in a fight. When nations are rivals it sometimes causes a war.

1 Germany against Britain
Rivalry between these Great Powers led to an arms race as it was called. The winner would be the nation which managed to build the strongest army and navy.

Britain was in the lead at the start because her navy was stronger. The German Emperor decided to build a larger navy than Britain had. The British didn't like this so they built an improved battleship

ACTIVITY

Get a photocopy of the map on page 8. Colour the nations which were Great

Source 1.4

The Royal Review or Inspection of the Navy at Spithead in 1901.

called HMS *Dreadnought*. It had ten 12-inch guns which could be fired on both sides of the ship. Germany then began to build ships of the same type as *Dreadnought*. Britain then added more dreadnoughts to her fleet. The race had started!

Source 1.5

Construction of British and German Dreadnoughts

The Naval Race

Dreadnoughts	Great Britain	Germany
1906	1	-
1907	3	-
1908	2	4
1909	2	3
1910	3	1
1911	5	3
1912	3	2
1913	7	3
1914	3	1
total	29	17
Dreadnought battle-cruisers		
1906	-	-
1907	3	-
1908	-	-
1909	1	-
1910	1	2
1911	2	1
1912	1	2
1913	1	2
1914	-	-
total	9	7

TALKING POINT

Britain had a huge navy. What was so wrong with Germany wanting one as well?

2 France against Germany

We've already seen that the French and Germans had fought against each other and that France had been defeated. Germany had taken Alsace-Lorraine from France. She had no intention of giving it back. The French wanted revenge but were afraid of the strong German army which would soon become the strongest in the world. France was afraid that Germany might take over some of the French Empire in Africa.

3 Russia against Austria-Hungary

Russia and Austria-Hungary had also been rivals for many years. Austria-Hungary wanted to influence and boss around the independent nations to the south-east of her. If you look at the map on p. 8 once again you will see these nations are called:

> Montenegro
> Serbia
> Bulgaria and
> Rumania

But these nations had links with Russia because the Russian people were similar to their people in many ways. So the Russian Emperor said he was their protector. He wanted to protect these small nations from Austria-Hungary and stop the Austrians bossing them about.

WORD FILE

Cartoon An amusing drawing which often makes fun of leaders or governments and what they do.

Empire Land outside the borders of a nation which has been taken over by that nation. Such lands are called colonies. Added together they make up an empire.

Independent A nation which rules itself, and so is not ruled by any other nation, is an independent nation.

Influence You have influence if you can force or persuade another person or another nation to do something.

Nation A large number of people who usually live in the same country. They usually speak the same language. They have been together for a long time and feel they belong together.

Power The strength and authority of a person or nation. It gives that person or nation influence over others.

Rivalry When two or more people or nations compete for a prize or for a good position in the world. Those who compete are called competitors or rivals.

Extension 1

Kaiser William II and his Germany

1 The French and British point of view

Source 1.6 shows what the French and British thought of Kaiser William II. He is shown posing for his portrait in the way he loved to stand. Here he is, in uniform, sword in hand, basking vainly in his own glory. He is hoping he'll have success at war.

The French and British governments believed he couldn't be trusted to use his power wisely. Why was he increasing the size of his army and navy? Why did he boast all the time about Germany being the greatest nation? Why did he demand a larger empire? All this showed that he wanted a war.

Source 1.6

A French Cartoon of Kaiser William II

Source 1.7

A British Cartoon from *Punch Magazine*. (The 'old song' was a favourite hit in British music halls)

COPYRIGHT EXPIRES.

GERMAN SAILOR. " WE DON'T WANT TO FIGHT, BUT, BY JINGO IF WE DO, WE'VE GOT THE SHIPS, WE'VE GOT THE MEN, WE'VE GOT THE MONEY TOO."
JOHN BULL. "I SAY, THAT'S *MY* OLD SONG."
GERMAN SAILOR. "WELL, IT'S *MINE* NOW."

2 The German point of view

The Germans took a very different point of view or opinion (see source 1.8). Historians have had a hard job deciding which of the two opinions is correct. Probably there is some truth in both but you must make up *your* mind. It is *your* opinion which matters.

Source 1.8

Extract from Surgeon with the Kaiser's Army **by Stephen Westman, William Kimber, 1968 (Adapted):**

    ❝ The Berliners enjoyed watching the big parades on the Tempelhofer Field and seeing the Kaiser on horseback standing under a tree, reviewing his troops. He was like a god, in the uniform of the Garde du Corps, with a silver helmet crowned with the Prussian Eagle. He rode in front. The people lined the streets and cried Hurrah! and the Kaiser saluted them with his field-marshal's baton, while he held the reins of his horse with his left hand, thus almost hiding his short and crippled left arm. The Kaiser's motto was, 'If you want peace, you must prepare for war'.. You must remember that his Empire had two very strong neighbours, Russia and revenge-seeking France, whose combined armies were at least double the strength of Germany's, and who had three million more soldiers.

The Germans had developed a highly efficient and rapidly expanding industry, for which they needed export markets and raw materials. Furthermore, Germany had grown enormously in population up to sixty-five millions; she needed an outlet for her population in the form of an Empire. She was late on the scene – Britain with only thirty-eight millions had her vast Empire; France, Belgium and Portugal, didn't have growing populations. Instead their populations were getting smaller but they were still trying to enlarge their African possessions.

So friction developed. France and Britain tried to stop any new nation getting hold of colonies. All they allowed Germany to have were a few stretches of land in Africa, mostly desert or jungle. This I think, was the approximate view of the ordinary peace-loving German. So William II's efforts to build a navy, which would be as strong as the British Battle Fleet, were understandable. **"**

ASSIGNMENTS

Use the source information and reference books where necessary.

1 Why did Kaiser William II display himself in the way described at 'big parades'?
2 What bodily handicap did the Kaiser have? Suggest a link there might have been between the handicap and his behaviour.
3 In what ways did the Kaiser carry out his motto and prepare for war in the 1890s?
4 What three points does the writer use to support what the Kaiser was doing?
5 Why is France described as 'revenge-seeking' in relation to Germany? Was there any truth in this?
6 Why was Germany 'late on the scene' in the race to get an empire?
7 'A few stretches of land in Africa'. Use a historical atlas to find out the names of

Germany's four African colonies.
8 Were the Kaiser's 'efforts to build a navy' to equal Britain's successful or not?

TALKING POINT

In view of this defence of what Kaiser William II was doing, should the British and French have let him get on with it?

Extension 2

The Naval Race: Great Britain against Germany

The start of the race
From 1898 Germany began to expand her navy. For centuries past Britain's navy had defended her Empire and 'ruled the waves'. The German challenge to British naval superiority was bound to cause alarm. So Britain began a programme of improvements to the Royal Navy. A new North Sea Fleet was based at a new naval port built at Rosyth, near Edinburgh. But the most important improvement was the design of H.M.S. *Dreadnought* (launched in 1906).

This advance in naval technology would have developed even if there had been no German challenge. It meant that all existing battleships were now out-of-date. But

Germany was also developing an advanced battleship, her own dreadnought.

So the naval race began again, almost from scratch. It was a race to see which nation could build the most dreadnoughts.

Source 1.9
HMS *Dreadnought* in dry dock

Armour plating	28 cm thick on the sides and 35 cm thick on the decks
Guns (firing on both sides)	28 (10 12-inch guns 18 4-inch guns)
Torpedo tubes	5
Speed	22 knots
Crew	860 sailors

13

Cartoon showing the British Naval Construction Programme and the German Naval Programme

King Edward VII to the Kaiser William II: 'Your little masterpiece is too ambitious. Keep it as a sketch.'

The German Challenge
Source 1.11 _____

Extract from The World Crisis **by W.S. Churchill (adapted)**

❝ With every rivet that von Tirpitz drove into his ships of war, he united British opinion ... in every walk of life and in every part of the Empire. The hammers that clanged at Kiel and Wilhelmshaven were forging the alliance of nations by which Germany was to be resisted and finally overthrown. ❞

The British Response
Source 1.12 _____

Extract from a letter of Lord Fisher to

Viscount Esher, 2 April 1912 (adapted):

❝ As you say, Winston Churchill has done splendidly. He and I last November discussed every brick of his speech in Devonport Dockyard while visiting the 33-knot *Lion* Dreadnought. He stopped dramatically on the dockyard stones and said to me, 'You're a great man!'

We are lagging behind in out-Dreadnoughting the Dreadnought! Now we want a Dreadnought that will go round the world without having to refuel.

Every little petty German newspaper is dead on for war with Britain! ... So anything would start a war! The heart of Winston's speech lies in these words.

'We must always be ready to meet at our average moment anything that any possible enemy might hurl against us at his selected moment.' ❞

ASSIGNMENTS

Use the source information and reference books, where necessary.

1 In what three major ways was H.M.S. *Dreadnought* superior to previous British battleships?
2 Why did the launching of H.M.S. *Dreadnought* mean the naval race started again almost from scratch?
3 Explain what the cartoon (source 1.10) is saying about the naval race. Is the cartoonist German or British? Give two reasons for your answer.
4 The Kaiser and the King were of course not directly responsible for their government's naval build-up. The sources refer to those who were:
   a) Von Tirpitz – what was his position in Germany?
   b) Lord Fisher – what was his position in Britain (1904–10) and why did Churchill regard him as a 'great man'?
   c) Winston Churchill – what office did he hold at this time (1911–15)?
5 What 'alliance of nations' is Churchill referring to in source 1.11? What is he saying about the formation of that alliance?
6 Refer to source 1.5. How ready was the Royal Navy to meet the enemy 'at his selected moment' in 1914? How did the German navy stand in comparison?

2 The Road to War

Alliances and 'Armed Camps'

You have seen that nations often behave like ordinary people. Just as people can become friends, nations can become allies. Sometimes allies strengthen their friendship by a written agreement called an *alliance*. When nations make an alliance they want the same things. You have seen there was rivalry among the nations in the 1890s. Each nation wanted help against its rival nation. So it made sense to get together to form alliances.

The building of alliances took many years to complete. By 1907 there were two great alliances in Europe, the Triple Alliance and the Triple Entente (a French word for alliance). Here are the nations which joined these alliances:

TRIPLE ALLIANCE	TRIPLE ENTENTE
GERMANY	GREAT BRITAIN
AUSTRIA-HUNGARY	FRANCE
ITALY	RUSSIA

Remember that some of these nations were taking part in an arms race. So Europe came to be divided into two armed alliances. In war, soldiers occupy camps and so historians write about the two 'armed camps'.

Any quarrel or argument between the two armed camps might lead to a war at any time. In the end such a quarrel led to the First World War. But the first few quarrels were patched up somehow and war was avoided.

 ACTIVITY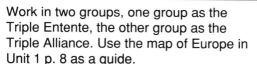

Work in two groups, one group as the Triple Entente, the other group as the Triple Alliance. Use the map of Europe in Unit 1 p. 8 as a guide.

Each group should draw and cut out shapes of its own nations to be stuck on a large map outline provided by the teacher. Then each group should colour its own nations in the same colour to indicate the two alliances.

Source 2.1 _____

A cartoonist's view of the Two Alliances

Use source 2.1 and the information you have been given.

1. Answer these questions correctly and so get safely across Europe.

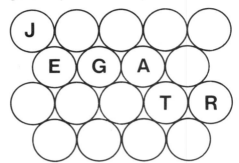

a) What J is the character standing for Britain?

b) What E is the name given to the alliance of 1904 between Britain and France?

c) What G is the nation shown by the man wearing a helmet?

d) What A is the nation shown by the man wearing two crowns?

e) What T is the name given to the alliance of the nations in the centre of Europe?

f) What R is the nation shown by the bear?

2. Which alliance is shown as more warlike?
Give a reason for your answer.

3. The Triple Alliance complained that it was in a circle surrounded by the Triple Entente. Was the complaint true? Give a reason for your answer.

Two Quarrels over Morocco

Quarrel One: In 1905 Morocco was one of the few independent nations left in Africa. France and Germany both wanted to increase their influence in Africa. Morocco gave them a chance to do this because the Sultan of Morocco was weak and could be controlled like a puppet.

France had the support of Britain at this time (see source *2.1*) through the *Entente Cordiale*. Germany believed this support was too weak to stop her having her way in Morocco, so in 1905 the Kaiser visited Tangier. He made a speech to declare that Morocco should not be taken over by any other nation.

This was clearly a challenge to France and Britain. They could not let the Germans interfere in Morocco like that. Although pride was hurt, the Great Powers drew back from going to war. A *conference* was held at Algeciras in Spain. The French and British stuck together and forced Germany to back down. The Kaiser had to recognise that France and not Germany was to act like a policeman over Morocco.

Quarrel Two: In 1911 the Sultan of Morocco called on his policeman, France, to help put down riots among his people. The French sent an army into Fez. An angry Germany replied by sending the gunboat *Panther* to the port of Agadir. Again it looked like war between Germany and France. But again Germany backed down when it was clear that Britain would join France if a war did start. Germany gave up her interest in Morocco in return for some land in the French Congo.

Morocco 1905–11

Source 2.2

German cartoon on the Agadir incident

Source 2.3

British cartoon on the Agadir incident

SOLID.

GERMANY. "IT'S ROCK. I THOUGHT IT WAS GOING TO BE PAPER."

WORK SECTION

Look at sources 2.2 and 2.3. Both cartoons are about power and the influence which power gives to a nation.

Answer the following questions:

1 Which nation is shown to be using its power?

2 Who is shown in source 2.2? Give his name and title.

3 How does the German cartoon (source 2.2) exaggerate what really happened?

Is it by:

a) putting the gunboat close to Agadir?

b) giving Germany an armoured fist on top of Agadir?

Give a reason for your answer.

4 How does the British cartoon (source 2.3) give a true picture of what really happened? In your answer use two out of these three statements.

| The Entente Cordiale stood firm |
| Germany was utterly defeated |
| Germany felt hurt and backed down |

The Balkans, 1890–1914

Quarrels over the Balkans

Look at the map. The shaded area is known as the Balkans. Long ago two Great Powers, Austria-Hungary and Turkey, had built empires here by taking over lands belonging to many national groups. These groups, such as the Slovaks, Bosnians and Albanians, wanted to become independent nations. There were also independent nations with some of their people living outside their borders. For example, there were Serbs living outside Serbia. The independent nations wanted to expand to include all their people within their

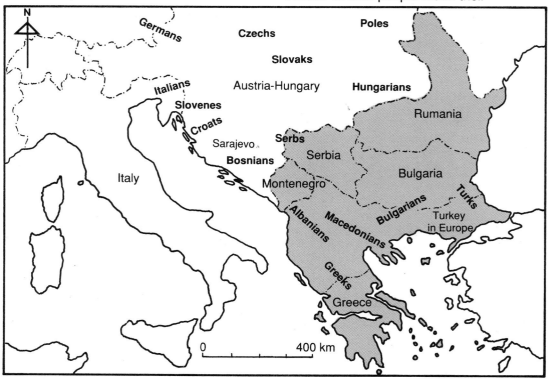

boundaries. There was bound to be trouble, sooner or later.

What about the Great Powers in or near the Balkans? The Turkish Empire was very weak and likely to collapse. Austria-Hungary, of the Triple Alliance, wanted to increase her own influence and prevent the national groups in her Empire from gaining their independence. Russia, of the Triple Entente, also wanted to extend her influence into the Balkans by helping the national groups gain their independence from Turkey and Austria-Hungary.

This situation brought about two Balkan Wars between 1912 and 1913. But during these years Austria-Hungary and Russia avoided being dragged in and so avoided a much bigger war between themselves.

The Assassination at Sarajevo

As you can see from the map of the Balkans (on p. 17), Sarajevo was a town in Austria-Hungary. It was in the province of Bosnia. Many Serbs lived in Bosnia and they wanted Bosnia to become part of Serbia.

On 28 June 1914, the heir to the throne of Austria-Hungary, Archduke Franz Ferdinand, arrived in Sarajevo with his wife, Sophie. It was a *State Visit* and the streets were crowded with sightseers.

In the crowd that day were six assassins who had plotted together to assassinate the Archduke. They were all Serbs. The Archduke drove in an open car along Appel Quay. He was dressed in military uniform, with his wife at his side. One of the

Source 2.4

Archduke Ferdinand and his wife, Sophie, at Sarajevo

Source 2.5

Map of the part of Sarajevo where the assassination took place

assassins threw a bomb at the car but it bounced off the folded roof and exploded in the street. Some sightseers were injured.

Later in the day the Archduke was driven back along the same street. The driver got confused about his route. He began to turn a corner and then slowed down and reversed. Another assassin who was standing near by pulled out a gun and fired at the Archduke at close range. The assassin's name was Gavrilo Princip.

Source 2.6

Gavrilo Princip

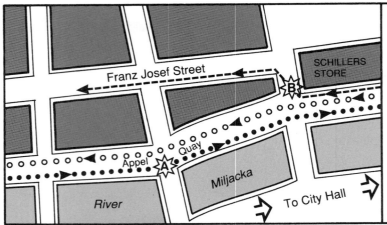

A Site of bomb attack
B Princip's successful attempt

•●▶•••••●▶•••
Franz Ferdinand's route to the City Hall

-◀--------◀--
Return route from City Hall as originally planned

o◀o o o o o o◀o o
Return route from City Hall as decided after the bomb attack

WORK SECTION

Use sources 2.4–2.6 and the information given to answer the following questions:

1. Who wanted Bosnia to become part of Serbia: the Bosnians living in Bosnia, the Serbs living in Bosnia or the Serbs living in Serbia?

2. Why did the assassins want to kill Archduke Franz Ferdinand?
Was it because he was:
   a) rich and powerful?
   b) a Roman Catholic?
   c) an Austrian by birth?
   d) the heir to the Austrian throne?
Copy the correct answer.

Source 2.7 _____

Account by Count Von Harrach who was in the front of the Archduke's car:

❝ As I was drawing out my handkerchief to wipe away the blood from the Archduke's lips, Her Highness cried out: 'For God's sake! What has happened to you?' Then she sank down from her seat with her face between the Archduke's knees. I had no idea that she had been hit and thought that she had fainted from shock. His Royal Highness said: 'Sophie, Sophie, don't die. Live for my children.' Thereupon I seized the Archduke by the coat collar to prevent his head from sinking forward and asked him: 'Is your Highness in great pain?' He clearly answered: 'It is nothing.' His face was slightly distorted, and he repeated six or seven times, every time losing more consciousness and with a fading voice: 'It is nothing.' The two unconscious bodies were carried into the governor's residence. The doctors examined them and said that they were already dead. ❞

Source 2.8 _____

Franz Ferdinand and Sophie in their coffins

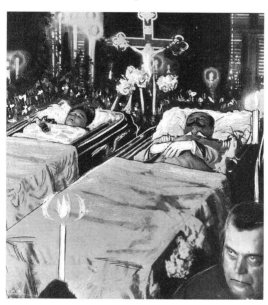

From Sarajevo to War

Just after Gavrilo Princip fired at the Archduke, he was arrested. When it was found out that he was a Serb, Austria-Hungary demanded revenge. The Serbian government was blamed for Princip's crime.

Once Austria-Hungary was certain that Germany would help her she decided to attack Serbia. But Russia was friendly to Serbia and began to move her armies to the borders of Austria-Hungary.

Source 2.9 _____

THE POWER BEHIND.

AUSTRIA (at the ultimatum stage). "I DON'T QUITE LIKE HIS ATTITUDE. SOMEBODY MUST BE BACKING HIM."

Source 2.9 shows the situation very well. In July Austria-Hungary declared war on Serbia. Now the whole network of alliances began to work and the two armed camps this time could not hold back from war. The First World War had begun.

Use source 2.9 and the information given to answer the following questions.

1 Which nation is the bear in the cartoon: Germany, Austria-Hungary, Russia or Britain?

2 What attitude does the Serbian cock display?

Choose from one of these words:

CONCEITED   ANGRY   DEFIANT

FRIGHTENED   FED-UP

3 Why can Serbia display such an attitude towards Austria-Hungary?

4 Which nation could the cartoonist have placed as the power behind Austria-Hungary: Germany, Russia, Britain or Turkey?

5 Copy the following and fill in the gaps correctly:
Austria-Hungary did not declare war on Serbia until she was sure that her main ally, _ _ _ _ _ _ _ _ would give support. The Serbs remained firm because they were sure of support from _ _ _ _ _ _. In the Triple _ _ _ _ _ _ _, Russia was allied to France and
_ _ _ _ _ _ _ _ _ _ _ _. Italy was also on the side of Austria-Hungary and Germany in the Triple _ _ _ _ _ _ _ but she decided to stay out of the quarrel. The pride of Austria-Hungary was hurt by the assassination at _ _ _ _ _ _ _ _ and this led directly to the
_ _ _ _ _ _ _ _ _ War.

TALKING POINT

In Sarajevo today Gavrilo Princip is respected as a hero. What do you think about assassins? Are they always criminals or always heroes?

WORD-FILE

Alliance   A friendship between two or more nations usually brought about by the signing of a written agreement.
Armed Camp   A nation or alliance of nations which is prepared for war.
Assassination   The murder of a leader of a nation or of some other important person. The victim is assassinated. The murderer is an assassin.
Conference   A meeting of leaders to discuss problems and other matters. The aim is to get everyone to agree.
Entente Cordiale   An alliance, signed in 1904, between Britain and France. The French words mean 'friendly understanding'.
State Visit   When a royal person or a leader of a government visits a place to be seen by the public. Crowds of sightseers line the streets. The opposite is a private visit without any fuss.

Extension 1

The Making of the Triple Entente

This Extension will help you to follow the various stages in the building up of the Triple Entente.

The first stage in the making of the Triple Entente was an alliance signed between France and Russia in 1894. Russia felt threatened by the Triple Alliance, signed in 1882, and so began to be more friendly towards France.

Stage 1 – Dual Alliance between Russia and France, 1894

Source 2.10 _____

Text of the terms of the Dual Alliance

❝ France and Russia, having no other aim than to meet the need of a defensive war, brought about by an attack of the forces of the Triple Alliance against one or other of them, have agreed upon the following provisions:
'If France is attacked by Germany, or by Italy supported by Germany, Russia shall employ all her available forces to attack Germany. If Russia is attacked by Germany, or by Austria-Hungary supported by Germany, France shall employ all her available forces to fight Germany'. ❞

1 What is meant by a 'defensive war'?
2 Do you agree that France and Russia had no other object than defence?
3 Which nation did France and Russia regard as the greatest threat to them?
4 Give reasons why the nations of the Triple Alliance had joined together?

Stage 2 – Entente Cordiale between Britain and France, 1904

This was an important change in Britain's relations with the outside world. For most of the nineteenth century Britain had felt no need to make alliances with other nations.

She had a great Empire which was well protected by a powerful navy. So she could afford to stand alone.

But now Britain felt the need to have an ally.

Source 2.11 _____

From War Memoirs **by D Lloyd George:**

❝ In the year 1904, on the day when the Anglo-French Entente was announced, I arrived at Dalmeny on a couple of days' visit to the late Lord Rosebery. His first greeting to me was: 'Well, I suppose you are just as pleased as the rest of them with this French agreement?' I assured him that I was delighted that our snarling and scratching relations with France had come to an end at last. He replied. 'You are all wrong. It means war with Germany in the end'.❞

Use the source information and reference books, where necessary.
1 Why, by 1904, did Britain feel the need to have an ally in the world?
2 'Our snarling and scratching relations with France'. Find out why there were bad relations between Britain and France between 1890 and 1903.
3 Find out what part King Edward VII played in improving his nation's relations with France.
4 Lord Rosebery was right in his prophecy that there would be war with Germany. Was he also right to believe that the signing of the Entente Cordiale would help to cause that war? Give reasons for your answer.

Stage 3 – Completion of the Triple Entente, 1907

In 1907, Russia (already, as you have seen, in alliance with France) signed an agreement with both Britain and France. This meant that Russia, France and Britain were now joined together in the Triple Entente.

1 Britain had become friendly with another nation, this time outside Europe. Which nation was this? (See cartoon below.)
2 What is France urging Russia to do with Britain?
3 What might Britain be accused of doing if it was 'treading on the toes' of other nations?
4 What had made it possible for France to say about Britain's John Bull: 'I find him adorable!'?

Source 2.12 _____

Cartoon from _Punch_ 11 October 1905

WHY NOT?

FRANCE (to RUSSIA). "AREN'T YOU GOING TO DANCE WITH MR. BULL?"
RUSSIA. "I THINK I SHOULD RATHER LIKE TO, IF HE WOULDN'T TREAD ON MY TOES."
FRANCE. "OH, BUT HE WON'T. HE'S IMPROVED IMMENSELY. I FIND HIM ADORABLE!"

Extension 2

The Balkan Wars and the Rise of Serbia

This Extension will show what Serbia gained from the two Balkan Wars to make her the most powerful of the Balkan nations. This angered Austria-Hungary and almost caused in 1912 and 1913 what at last happened in 1914 – a great European war.

The Balkan League: In 1912 yet another alliance was formed in Europe. Serbia, Greece, Bulgaria and Montenegro joined together in the Balkan League.

The First Balkan War 1912: The new alliance felt strong enough to attack Turkey which, as we have seen, was very weak.

In a short war of seven weeks the Turks were almost entirely driven out of Europe. In the War Serbia had taken the lead and had shown herself to be the strongest state of the Balkan League.

Austria-Hungary was very upset by these events. If the Turkish Empire was so quickly destroyed, perhaps the Austrian Empire would share the same fate. Serbia should be taught a lesson. But Serbia was supported by Russia. If Russia attacked Austria-Hungary, Germany would support the Austrians and France and Britain would support Russia. The outcome would be a European war. The Great Powers drew back from this horror and forced a peace settlement on the Balkan League. The lands taken over from Turkey were divided between the nations of the Balkan League. But Austria-Hungary insisted that the Albanians should be made into an independent nation. The new Albania blocked Serbia's path to the sea.

The 2nd Balkan War 1913: Bulgaria quarrelled with Serbia and Greece over the division of Turkish lands. An even shorter war (of four weeks) followed. Bulgaria was defeated and was forced to give up most of the lands she had won in the First War to Greece and Serbia.

Serbia was stronger than ever! She had doubled her size and proved that she could fight and win wars.

Source 2.14

Report of a German journalist, 18 November 1912 (adapted):

❝ There are no illusions about the importance of events in the Balkans for the future of the Austrian Empire. With amazement and worry we watch the sudden surge of Serbia and on all lips is the worried question: what is to become of Austria-Hungary? Will it be

Source 2.13

a) The Balkans in 1912 before the Balkan Wars

b) The Balkans in 1913 after the Balkan Wars

possible to keep the seven million Southern Slavs within the Empire if the government doesn't take vigorous action against Serbian claims? **"**

Source 2.15 _____

From a speech of the Serbian Prime Minister, Nikola Pasic, after the Second Balkan War:

" The first round is won: now we must prepare for the second round, against Austria-Hungary. **"**

ASSIGNMENTS

Use the source information and reference books, where necessary.

1 Which Empire lost most of its lands in Europe?
2 How were these lands lost and why were they lost so easily?
3 Which Balkan nation extended its lands the most?
4 Which new nation gained its independence after the Second Balkan War?
5 How and why was this brought about?
6 Give reasons why Austria-Hungary was alarmed by 'the sudden surge of Serbia'?
7 Which of the two written sources gives the more convincing proof that Austria-Hungary was in some danger from Serbia (sources 2.14 and 2.15)? Give a reason for your answer.
8 Why would a German watch the events in the Balkans 'with amazement and worry'?

3 Men and Machines of War

The Nations at War

As the name The First World War suggests, the *conflict* which began in August 1914 involved many nations. At the start all the nations of the Triple Alliance except Italy fought all the nations of the Triple Entente. Japan had already made an alliance with Britain and quickly joined the War.

Soon other nations joined in. Italy changed sides and joined Britain and France. Much later these nations were joined by the United States of America. Turkey fought on the German side.

Only a few nations were *neutral* in the War. One neutral nation – Belgium – was forced into the conflict.

The Invasion of Belgium

Long before 1914 the Germans had worked on a plan for a future war on two *fronts*. One front was against France to the West. The other front was against Russia to the East. It was called the Schlieffen Plan. It aimed to get a quick victory over France, quick enough for the German armies to turn eastwards and then fight the Russians.

A quick victory could not be gained by attacking the frontier between Germany and France which was well-defended. So the German plan had to find an easier and quicker route.

In August 1914 Germany asked Belgium to let the German army through. Belgium refused. Britain sent a warning to Germany that the British had an agreement to defend Belgium's position as a neutral. The Germans took no notice and invaded Belgium.

Britain declared war on Germany and sent the *British Expeditionary Force* (B.E.F.) to help the French.

The Belgians fought hard against the Germans and slowed down their advance towards France. When they got into France

the British and French armies stopped them reaching Paris. The Schlieffen Plan had failed.

Source 3.1

This cartoon gives a true picture of the British viewpoint of events in August 1914

BRAVO, BELGIUM!

 **WORK SECTION**

Answer the following questions:
1 Why did the Germans plan to go through Belgium in order to attack France?
2 Which of these reasons tells us why

Britain went to war after the German invasion of Belgium?
Because Belgium was an ally.
Because Belgium was a small nation.
Because Belgium was a neutral nation.
Because Belgium was a kingdom.

3 Which of the words in blocks makes a sentence to tell us what the cartoon (source 3.1) is saying?
a) RUSSIA GERMANY FRANCE is going to invade Belgium.
b) Germany is behaving towards Belgium like a BULLY FRIEND GUIDE
c) Belgium is behaving WISELY BRAVELY STUPIDLY towards Germany.

4 Why wouldn't a German have agreed with the cartoonist about the events of August 1914?

5 If you had been a British citizen alive in 1914, what would the cartoon have encouraged you to do?

Trench Warfare

Both sides refused to give way at positions north of the River Marne (see map). They then raced northwards towards the sea, each trying to get round the other. Both reached the sea at the same time. They then held their positions by digging lines of trenches. Before long the trenches stretched right across France and Belgium (see map).

The aim of both sides was now to tire each other out by constantly attacking

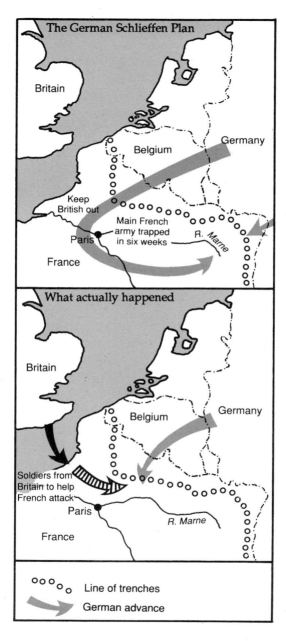

The German Schlieffen Plan

Britain
Belgium
Germany
Keep British out
Main French army trapped in six weeks
R. Marne
Paris
France

What actually happened

Britain
Belgium
Germany
Soldiers from Britain to help French attack
Paris
R. Marne
France

ooooo Line of trenches

→ German advance

1 The trenches were dug in zig-zag fashion.
2 There were three parallel lines, X, Y, Z. You could walk between them by the communication trenches marked W.

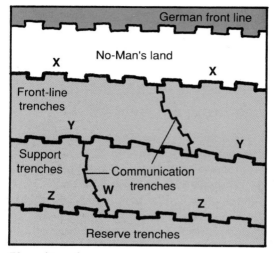

German front line
No-Man's land
X   X
Front-line trenches
Y   Y
Support trenches   Communication trenches
Z   W   Z
Reserve trenches

Plan of trenches

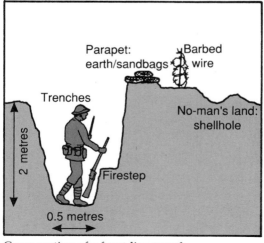

Parapet: earth/sandbags   Barbed wire
Trenches
No-man's land: shellhole
2 metres
Firestep
0.5 metres

Cross-section of a front-line trench

across the area between the two lines of trenches called *'No Man's Land'*. They hoped to break through the other side's trenches.

Larger scale attacks also occurred from time to time. These were the great battles of the First World War such as the Battle of the Somme in 1916. But until 1918 both sides managed to stop attacks breaking through their lines of trenches.

Fighting in the Trenches

It was against orders for the soldiers to write diaries. But many did. Other soldiers wrote down what they remembered after the War was over (memoirs). These writings give us information on what conditions were really like. Other useful sources of information are photographs and cartoons.

Source 3.2 _____

The Long Carry, **the War Diary of Stretcher Bearer Frank Dunham:**

❝ PARAPET and FIRING STEP: The sentries stood on a *firing step* and looked over the *parapet* during the night. They were not allowed to 'stand down' in the morning until the order had been given by the officer in charge. (17 Feb. 1917)

PERISCOPE: In the morning I had a walk down the front-line trench, just to see what it was like. I was tall so I had to stoop very low, so as not to provide a target for a Fritz sniper*. It was interesting

to peep through a *periscope*. I could see our own barbed wire and Jerry's barbed wire. I could also see the German front line in places. The top of the periscope had to stick up above the trench. (17 Dec. 1916)

CLOSENESS OF ENEMY: Quite near to our dugout the German trench ran close to ours, and on still nights we could hear the Germans walking on their *duckboards* and talking to their comrades. (17 Dec. 1916) **❞**

* Fritz sniper - German rifleman.

Source 3.3 _____

A Front-line Trench at Ovillers, July 1916

Source 3.4 _____

Cartoon by Bruce Bairnsfather *My Dug Out*

Source 3.5 _____

A Sergeant-Major's War – **the Diary of Ernest Shephard**

❝ SANDBAGS: The trenches are falling in at several places after only a short period of continual rain. Only one thing is any good to help improve matters and that is sandbags. These, filled with earth and started with a good foundation, will hold out and keep the sides of the trench from slipping in. The use of sandbags is essential for comfort and safety. (3 Nov. 1915)

MINES: Under the whole place there are mines. We ourselves are preparing eight separate mines, and the enemy is doing the same, probably more. We can hear them digging under us. (10 Aug. 1915)

SHELLS; Most shells give a fair warning. Jack Johnsons* give quite 45 seconds, and the lighter guns less. These high explosives give about three seconds, but a shell we call the whizz-bang gives no warning at all, simply like its name. (10 Mar. 1915)

BARBED WIRE: I looked carefully at our front-line trench as I have to put out wire tonight . . . At 9 pm a party of C Company arrived with wiring material. We started wiring from the road on the left across the gap. Very cold, dark night. We put out 120 yards [110 m] of wire 9 yards [8 m] deep, good work, finished at 2 am on Thursday 7th. (6 Dec. 1916)🙿

* Jack Johnsons – Nickname for a shell after a black heavyweight boxer. They were also called 'coal boxes'.

WORK SECTION

1 Look at sources 3.2 and 3.5 from soldiers' diaries and then source 3.6 from a soldier's memoirs. Why do you think diaries are usually more reliable than memoirs for learning history?

2 Why was it against orders for soldiers to keep diaries?

3 How high did a trench have to be?

4 Why was a periscope useful to a front-line soldier?

5 Copy a sentence from source 3.2 and another from source 3.5 to show that the British and German trenches were quite close. What was the ground between them called?

6 Two of the following from source 3.5 protected the trench parapet – sandbags, mines, shells, barbed wire. Which?

7 Would it be easier to dodge a whizz-bang or a 'Jack Johnson' (source 3.5)? Give a reason.

8 Which of the following can you see in source 3.3 – periscope, firing step, duckboard, sandbags, parapet, mine, barbed wire?

New Weapons

Every front-line soldier was armed with a rifle. A well trained rifleman could fire ten bullets every minute. Hand grenades (light bombs which were thrown by hand) were also used. The front-line soldier was backed up by the *artillery* which fired shells over the heads of soldiers in the trenches.

All these weapons had been used in other wars. In the First World War new and deadlier weapons were invented.

Source 3.6 _____

With a Machine Gun to Cambrai by George Coppard:

❝ MACHINE GUNS: Two Vickers machine guns were now issued to the battalion. The Vickers .303 water-cooled gun was a wonderful weapon, and its successful use led to the eventual formation of the Machine Gun Corps. . . The tripod was the heaviest part. The rate of fire could be well over 600 bullets every minute and when the gun was firmly fixed on the tripod it didn't move much and so could be aimed accurately.

TANKS: The tanks looked like giant toads against the skyline. Some of the leading tanks carried huge bundles of tightly-bound wood. These were dropped when a wide trench was reached and made a firm bridge to cross over . . . We went forward into enemy country in a way that would not have been possible without the help of tanks. The tanks appeared to have busted through every resistance. The enemy wire had been dragged about like old curtains.❞

Source 3.7 _____

British tank at Battle of Cambrai

Source 3.8

Johnny Get Your Gun **by John Tucker:**

❝ GAS: Gas shelling was now becoming very heavy, causing many casualties. You could detect gas not only from the strange 'plop' noise of the explosion, but also from the strong smell which hung around long after the shell had fallen. The gas affected the eyes, often causing temporary blindness. The nose, throat and lungs and any part of the body damp from sweat was affected as well. It caused soreness with red and inflamed patches. We often had to put on our gas-masks which made breathing difficult by mouth through the tube. ❞

Source 3.9

Soldiers in gas masks using Vickers Machine Gun

WORK SECTION

1 How many times faster was the firing rate of a machine gun than a rifle?
2 Why did the machine gun get hot and how was it kept cool?
3 Source 3.6 describes two things which a tank could do to help our soldiers. Copy these two things from the list below:
   It could cross wide trenches.
   It could give off poison gas.
   It could destroy enemy wire.
   It could construct trenches.
4 What was the bundle of wood on top of the tank used for?
5 How did a tank move without wheels?
6 What did soldiers do to protect themselves from a gas attack?

7 How did the wind sometimes make gas a useless weapon?
8 Which weapon in the blocks below would kill the most Germans if they were attacking in great numbers and moving across No Man's Land?

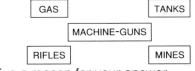

GAS		TANKS
	MACHINE-GUNS	
RIFLES		MINES

Give a reason for your answer.

BRITONS

"WANTS"

YOU

JOIN YOUR COUNTRY'S ARMY!

GOD SAVE THE KING

Life in the Trenches

Those who joined the army (called *enlisting*) were mainly volunteers. In the early months of the War men rushed to enlist. Boys pretended they were 19 years old, the minimum age, because they were so keen to enlist. Recruiting posters appeared to remind men of their duty. One of the posters showed the face and pointing finger of Lord Kitchener. He was the government minister in charge of the army. As the War went on many more men were needed to replace the huge number who were killed. So in 1916 enlistment was made compulsory for all fit men between 19 and 38 years old. Some men refused to fight because they didn't believe in killing. They were called Conscientious Objectors.

Once these keen recruits were trained and sent to the trenches, they soon lost their enthusiasm for war. Most of the time life was boring with harsh discipline and hard work. Every soldier was also in great danger when fighting in the front-line trenches.

Anyway most soldiers just had to put up with it like 'Old Bill' and his friend in the cartoon below. It was drawn by Captain Bruce Bairnsfather. His comic soldier, 'Old Bill', on the left, was a popular character in his cartoons.

The next few sources tell us what life in the trenches was like in the words of the soldiers themselves.

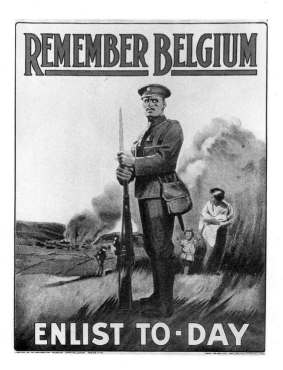

REMEMBER BELGIUM

ENLIST TO·DAY

LINE UP, BOYS!

ENLIST TO-DAY.

"Well, if you knows of a better 'ole, go to it."

Source 3.10

Cannon Fodder by A. Stuart Dolden (pub. 1980):

❝ RAIN & MUD: Everywhere the mud was deep, and in most cases came over your ankles. The rain eased off a little, so I made myself a shelter by covering a shell hole with my ground sheet... the rain began to fall again, so I went back to my shelter, where I found that a little dog had settled in my absence. He was shivering so much and looked so miserable, that I let him stay and we both curled up together. The rain pelted down during the night and I was bitterly cold. The little dog shivered and crept closer to me. A little way off I could see our cooker standing in a sea of mud... ❞

Source 3.11

The Long Carry, the War Diary of Stretcher-Bearer Frank Dunham:

❝ TRENCH FEET 23 Nov. 1916: Because of the mud in the trenches, we were all given rubber waders. It was a crime to get 'trench feet', and everyone was expected to rub his feet daily with whale oil and have clean dry socks to change into.

RATS 30 Nov. 1916: This camp was famous for its rats which must have lived on our rations. I remember one night being wakened by a rat running over my face, and could hear them sniffing away at a parcel of food I had received from home. They would scurry off when they were disturbed, but would return when everything was quiet again... It became usual for us all to sleep with our heads under the blankets, after one chap had his nose bitten by a rat.

LICE 21 Nov. 1916: While standing over a shell-hole full of water and rolling down my shirt at the neck to wash, I noticed lice on my vest for the first time. I was upset but I knew it had to come sooner or later, because the blankets which were given out were also full of lice. ❞

Source 3.12

On duty in a front-line trench

Source 3.13

Front-line trench

Source 3.14

All For a Shilling A Day **by Gunner William Pressey (extracts in** People at War **pub. 1973):**

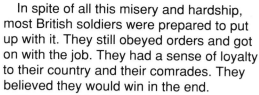

HUNGER: My whole four years as a gunner I was hungry all the time. Our actual rations were only about half what they should have been. If anyone had questioned the authorities they would have been told that every soldier got half a loaf of bread a day. We never got this once. Many times we had one slice only for breakfast and for tea hard biscuits. These were so hard that you had to put them on a firm surface and smash them with a stone or something.

DISCIPLINE: If a man was sentenced to No 1 Field Punishment he was tied or strapped to a gun wheel or wagon wheel. Legs spread out and ankles fastened to spokes of the wheel and the same with wrists... I had to help strap this man on. It was a freezing cold winter's day and we let him have an overcoat, balaclava helmet and woollen gloves. But half an hour later this Major strolled round, bellowed like a bull and ordered the overcoat, helmet and gloves to be removed. The man was there for an hour and a half and no one was allowed to speak to him or go near him. It took two chaps to fetch him in. He was almost frozen and we practically carried him back.

DEATH: Our arms caught him as he landed, and we lowered him into the bottom of the trench. He had been hit in the back, and in seconds his face turned black and he was dead. No one spoke. We turned away from each other to hide the tears. I am still crying as I write this. He was a grand lad and a good soldier and the shock of losing him lasted a long time. We would laugh at his jokes no more. Losing him seemed like losing a brother.

Source 3.15

Cheerful soldiers, July 1916

In spite of all this misery and hardship, most British soldiers were prepared to put up with it. They still obeyed orders and got on with the job. They had a sense of loyalty to their country and their comrades. They believed they would win in the end.

They could look forward to leave and rest periods away from the front line.

Their sense of humour also helped to keep their spirits up – funny nicknames for places and people, street names for trenches like 'Princes Street' and most of all made up songs of their own.

Here is an example, to the tune, 'Hold your hand out you naughty boy':

> Get yer head down, Fritzy boy,
> Get yer head down, Fritzy boy.
> Last night in the pale moonlight
> We saw yer, we saw yer.
> You was mending the broken wire
> When we opened with rapid fire.
> If you want to see yer father and yer fatherland,
> Get yer head down, Fritzy boy!

WORK SECTION

1 Copy the following half-completed sentences and try to complete them using evidence from the sources.
   a) Rats got fat by living on _ _ _ _ _ _ _
   b) Soldiers try to avoid trench feet by
      _ _ _ _ _ _ _ _ _ _ _
   c) Soldiers could not be blamed for having lice because _ _ _ _ _
   d) Often soldiers were hungry because
      _ _ _ _ _ _ _

2 What are the soldiers in source 3.12 doing?
3 Look at sources 3.12 and 3.13. Which of the two photographs better illustrates the conditions described in source 3.10? Give reasons for your answer.
4 Why are the soldiers in source 3.15 looking so cheerful?

The Battle of the Somme

The only way to break the *deadlock* of trench warfare was to start a large-scale attack on the Germans. These attacks (called offensives) had been tried before by both sides. But they had always failed. Both sides had held firm, stopping a breakthrough of the enemy's lines.

In the summer of 1916, the British Commander-in-Chief, Field Marshal Haig, decided to begin another offensive. The British and French agreed that the offensive should be in the area of the River Somme.

Haig's aim was to break through the

German trenches and force the Germans to retreat. Haig also wanted to kill as many Germans as possible.

Before the battle began the British artillery started up a tremendous bombardment of enemy positions. The big guns went on firing for seven whole days. The noise was heard in London! The guns should have smashed the German trenches, destroyed their barbed wire and silenced their machine guns and artillery. But this didn't happen as planned.

After the bombardment the Battle of the Somme began on 1 July 1916. Thousands of British troops climbed out of their trenches and attacked across No Man's Land. But they found that the German defences were still there. They crossed No Man's Land and were slaughtered. On the first day of the Battle of the Somme the British had almost 60 000 casualties, which means men killed, wounded or missing. It was the worst day in the history of the British Army.

The Battle went on until the middle of November, 1916. It was a dreadful disaster. The total British and French casualties added up to about 630 000 and the German casualties were about 660 000. The amount of ground gained by the Allies measured about 39 kilometres wide and a maximum of 8 kilometres in depth.

After all that slaughter both sides went back again to trench warfare.

TALKING POINT

What attitude would *we* have had to the War? Would we have been Conscientious Objectors, loyal soldiers or deserters?

 ACTIVITIES

1 Design a recruiting poster of your own.
2 Imagine you are a soldier fighting in the trenches. Make a cover for the diary you decide to write. Then write up an entry for the day 2 November 1915. Remember some of the bad conditions you are suffering.
3 Make a model from papier mache to show the lay-out of British and German trenches, No Man's Land and the position of artillery and machine guns.
4 Look for examples of songs from the First World War. Copy and learn one which you like.

WORD-FILE

Artillery   The large guns of an army. Also the division of the army which uses them.
British Expeditionary Force   The British Army serving in France and Belgium. Called the B.E.F. for short.
Conflict   Any kind of fight or struggle.
Duckboards   Wooden slats placed in the bottom of trenches to cover water or mud.
Deadlock   Complete standstill or lack of any progress.
Enlisting   Recruiting men for the army and navy. The enlisted men took an oath of loyalty and were given 'the King's shilling' as a token.
Firing Step   A step hollowed out in the side of a trench for soldiers to stand on when firing. It was high enough to allow them to see over the parapet.
Front   Line of an army nearest the enemy. The Western Front was in France and Belgium. There were other fronts in the War.
Neutral   A nation or a person who refuses to take sides in a war or other type of conflict.
No Man's Land   The ground between the German and Allied trenches which belonged to neither side.
Parapet   The mound along the top of the side of the trench which faces the enemy.
Periscope   A tube with mirrors which allows a person in a low position or under water to see things otherwise out of sight.

Extension 1

The Failure of the Schlieffen Plan

This Extension will help you to revise what has already been learned about the Schlieffen Plan. It will give you a fuller understanding of how and why the Plan failed.

Remember that the Germans aimed to avoid fighting France and Russia at the same time. So France must be defeated before the Russians could move against Germany in the east. Everything depended on speed and so the quickest route to Paris was chosen – through neutral Belgium. Although the B.E.F. failed to halt the German advance at Mons and began to retreat with their French allies towards Paris, the Plan failed. It failed partly because of what happened in Belgium and partly because of the victory of the Allies at the Battle of the Marne.

Source 3.16 _____

Extracts from Forty Days in 1914 **by Maj.-Gen. Sir F. Maurice (adapted) (pub. 1918):**

❝ The Germans were convinced that their plan was the only safe one and that questions of right and wrong did not matter. Germany was quite determined to march through Belgium. It is not my purpose to describe in any detail the German campaign of frightfulness in Belgium. The savagery with which it was conducted has been put down to such causes as exasperation at the heavy losses suffered in the capture of Liege, the natural brutality of the German soldiers, and anger at the cheek of little Belgium in daring to resist the commands of the War Lord of Europe. The savagery was an element in the scheme to save the time which was so precious and to secure by terrorism the uninterrupted march of the main forces to their goal. **"**

Source 3.17 _____

Von Moltke's Order of the Day, 5 Sept. 1914:

" The enemy has managed to avoid being surrounded by the attacks of the 1st and 2nd armies and has reached the neighbourhood of Paris with parts of his forces. It must be reckoned that the enemy is assembling strong forces in the neighbourhood of Paris for the protection of the capital and to threaten the right flank of the German Armies. **"**

Source 3.18 _____

Joffre's Order of the Day, 6 Sept. 1914:

" Every effort must be made to attack and throw back the enemy. A unit which can no longer advance must at all costs retain the ground it has gained, and rather than retire, be killed on the spot. In the present circumstances no weakness can be tolerated. **"**

34

Use the source information and reference books where necessary.

1 Study the maps on p. 25. Make a sketch map of your own to show what happened in 1914. Add to the map Liege, Ypres and Mons in Belgium. Draw four arrows instead of the one shown to mark the advance of the four German armies. Draw a line to mark the limit of their advance instead of the line showing the trenches.
2 Why were there 'questions of right and wrong' about the course of the Schlieffen Plan?
3 Why was it so important to capture Liege? What happened there in August 1914?
4 Find examples of German savagery or 'frightfulness' in Belgium.
5 The British and French newspapers deliberately exaggerated reports of how the Germans treated the Belgians. What words in source 3.16 suggest that Maj.-Gen. Maurice's account may be exaggerated?
6 Who was 'the War Lord of Europe'? Give reasons why you agree or disagree with this description.
7 Who were Von Moltke and Joffre?
8 Was Von Moltke correct in his reckoning of likely French action in the Paris area? How did the Commandant of Paris rush the Paris garrison to the scene of fighting? (A colourful incident of the War.)
9 What battle began in Sept. 1914 and were the forces of Joffre and his British Allies successful in 'throwing back the enemy'?
10 What reasons would you give for the failure of the Schlieffen Plan?

_____

Extension 2

_____

The 'Big Push' on the Somme, *July–Nov., 1916*

This Extension will help you find out more about the Battle of the Somme using the evidence of soldiers who were there.

Source 3.19 _____

Extracts from With a Machine Gun to Cambrai **by George Coppard (adapted):**

" The British and French attack was designed to relieve heavy German pressure on Verdun in the south. 26 divisions were British and 14 were French, and the total territory gained during the whole of the Somme battle was about eighty square kilometres. For this miserable fraction of the earth's surface about three-quarters of a million British and French soldiers became casualties.

On the afternoon of 1 July, a date that will never be forgotten, we passed through Albert on our way to the front, and we knew that the great attack had started early that morning.

The next morning we gunners surveyed the dreadful scene in front of our trench. Immediately in front was clear evidence that the attack had been brutally repulsed. Hundreds of dead were strung out like wreckage washed up. Quite as many died on the enemy wire as on the ground, like fish caught in a net.

Many of the wounded were out there in front of us, and their cries for help continued for days. **"**

Source 3.20 _____

Extracts from the Diary of Ernest Shephard, A Sergeant-Major's War:

" *2 July 1916*: Our men say the Germans fought very bravely. Also, they say enemy trenches were solidly built and needed nothing. Good dug-outs fitted luxuriously with electric lights, boarded and even wall-papered, plenty of good food, cigars, wines, in fact everything required. Plenty of German helmets as souvenirs. Enemy trenches choked with their own dead.

22 Nov. 1916: The battalion paraded and marched off at 1.30 pm. We marched through Northumberland Avenue to Mesnil. Very badly smashed. At the top of Mesnil Hill we had a splendid view of the captured country to Thiepval and the valley of the River Ancre.

After hours of waiting we moved into the German dug-outs in their old front line. Dug-outs not at all good, merely long corridors 6 feet [1.8 m] high, 3 feet 6 inches [.9 m] broad. **"**

ASSIGNMENTS

Use the source information and reference books where necessary.

1 In source 3.19 Coppard states one aim of the British and French at the Battle of the Somme. Give another important aim.
2 What was the 'clear evidence' that the attack had gone badly?
3 What should have destroyed the enemy barbed wire?
4 What evidence is provided in source 3.20 to show that some of Ernest Shephard's comrades had done well on the first day of the Battle?
5 What sentence shows that the Germans didn't always have comfortable living quarters in their trenches?
6 What was Northumberland Avenue likely to have been?
7 Which of the two diary entries is likely to give us a more reliable account of the success of Shephard's comrades in the Battle of the Somme? Give a reason for your answer.

4 The Home Fronts

The War at Home

All the nations in the War had a home front in addition to the fronts where their soldiers, sailors and airmen were fighting. The words 'home front' remind us that people who weren't fighting (called *civilians*) were still affected by the War. Civilians were expected to play their part in helping the Government win the War. We shall look at the home fronts in Britain and Germany.

WHAT YOU WILL LEARN

Unit 4 will help you to understand:
1 How civilians in Britain and Germany were controlled by their governments.
2 How people's lives were affected by this control.
3 How the civilians of Britain and Germany helped their governments try to win the War.
4 The effect of bombing raids on the people of Britain.
5 What British and German civilians felt and believed about the War.

The British and German Governments

There was a big difference in the way Britain and Germany were governed. Both had Parliaments elected by adult male voters. Britain's King and Government had to obey the British Parliament. But Germany's Emperor, the Kaiser, did not have to obey *his* Parliament. So in wartime, the Kaiser could carry on as before. He didn't need any special new orders to control the German Parliament.

Defence of the Realm Act
The British Government believed it couldn't win the War unless it controlled Parliament in the same way as the Kaiser did in Germany. Parliament agreed it was a good idea. So it passed the Defence of the Realm Act. It was called DORA for short.

This new law gave power to the Government to make any orders it thought necessary while the War lasted. It also said that people who didn't obey such orders would be tried in special courts. These courts had a judge but no jury. Punishments were severe.

Let's now look at some of these orders which took away much of the freedom people had in peacetime.

Censorship
One important freedom in Britain in peacetime is the freedom of newspapers to print what they like. But during the War the Government censored newspapers and, in some cases, letters and telegrams as well.

The censor examined newspapers before they were printed and removed from them any information thought to be useful to the enemy. Any information which might cause civilians to despair or panic was also censored. The Government issued its own news in *official bulletins*.

Source 4.1 _____

Extract from the Diary of the Rev. A. Clark:

❝ *20 March 1915*: A Leven (Fife) lady – an officer's wife – received a letter like this from her husband:
Blotted out (Presumably Place and Date) page 1 Dearest Wife, All the rest blotted out.
page 2 All blotted out.
page 3 All blotted out.
page 4 All blotted out except, Your devoted Tom.
Enclosed is their note: 'Madam, Your husband is quite well but has much too much to say signed, Censor'.
15 January 1916: 5.30 pm Miss Edith Caldwell called. She brought the envelope, stamped 'opened by Censor', of a letter from my daughter Mildred. Major Caldwell says this is the first time he has seen a letter opened by the censor, posted in this country to a home address.
25 November 1916: 7 pm Major James Caldwell called. He was very depressed about the War – rather an unusual thing for him. He hears from officers on leave that the official bulletins censor important facts, if they are unfavourable. Thus they

say there are 600 German prisoners at a particular position but say nothing of 20 000 British casualties in taking it. Nearly all the newspapers accept the Government's wish to hush up our army's losses. **„**

Propaganda

In addition to censoring or blotting out information that the Government didn't want people to know, the Government tried to make people believe what they wanted them to believe. In other words it put out leaflets, posters, films and stories for newspapers which weren't always strictly truthful. There was usually a grain of truth which was then exaggerated. This is called *propaganda*.

One type of propaganda was to make the Germans and the Kaiser look ridiculous. Another made out that the Germans were evil, inhuman monsters.

Newspapers and magazines often liked to put out their own propaganda of this kind.

The Germans used propaganda in their country against the British.

Source 4.2

Examples of propaganda

A   Front page of the *Daily Mirror*, Saturday, 19 Dec. 1914

B   German Poster (with translation below)

He's the cause! Why are we still fighting and dying? Why do we still have to scrimp and save? Why are our coal and light rationed? Why is our whole life controlled by rationing? Why can't we go about our ordinary work in peace? Because England is our deadly enemy. Therefore Forward Together! Forward in Strength! Then we can guarantee Victory for Germany.

C   British official war poster kept by the Rev. A. Clark. 'Kultur' is a word used by the Germans to describe their advanced standards in science, art and behaviour

Answer the following questions, using sources 4.1 and 4.2 to help you:

1 Why did the Censor blot out so much from the officer's letter to the lady in Leven?
2 Which of the Diary extracts (source 4.1) gives evidence that it wasn't only soldiers' letters which were censored.
3 Why did official bulletins and most newspapers 'hush up losses'?
4 Copy the following statements which apply to source 4.2. Label each one either 'True' or 'False':
   A is propaganda against the Germans
   B is propaganda against the Germans
   C is propaganda against the British
5 Both A and C in source 4.2 tell a story. Which is more likely to be a true story? Give two reasons for your answer.
6 What are A and C trying to make the reader believe?
7 Copy this list which applies to A in source 4.2. Then put a cross against those statements which you think exaggerate or distort the newspaper story:
   Murdered by the Kaiser
   Berlin rings joy bells
   Circulation larger than any other
   England's East Coast
   Butchery of these British babes

Trade Unions during the War

The freedom of workers to go on *strike* was another freedom which was done away with during the War. Strikes are organised by Trade Unions. They order all their members to stop working in the hope of forcing their bosses to give more pay or better conditions. There had been strikes in some parts of Britain from the earliest days of the War. The worst trouble spots were the South Wales coalfields and Clydeside in Scotland. Clydeside was called 'Red Clydeside' at this time because the people there were nearly all supporters of either the Labour Party or the Communist Party. Both Parties had red as their colour.

The Government felt that the workers shouldn't be allowed to strike while other workers, as soldiers, were risking their lives for very low pay in the trenches. So by a special law passed in 1915, strikes were banned by those industries making weapons and ammunition for the War, called the *munitions* industries. The law helped to prevent strikes but did not stop them altogether.

Trade Union leaders disliked the ban on strikes. They thought it was an attack on the rights of the workers. On Clydeside there was a big strike between March and April 1916 at the Parkhead Forge led by David Kirkwood. The Government stopped the strike and ten of the leaders, including Kirkwood, were arrested and forced to live outside the Glasgow–Clydeside area.

Source 4.3

From Johnny Get Your Gun **by John F. Tucker (pub. 1978):**

❝ One of the worst pieces of news to us was that of the strike by coal miners in England. This really did shock and disgust us. We, including many of these miners' sons and relatives, were sacrificing our lives and limbs to shield the British people from slavery or worse. These strikes were deliberately holding up the manufacture of weapons and ammunition as well as fuel for our naval and merchant ships. Many of us will never forgive or forget that betrayal. However badly the miners were paid at that time, others were sacrificing themselves getting a tiny sum of a very few shillings a week. The time to strike is not when the country is in danger.❞

Source 4.4

From the War Memoirs of David Lloyd George, **(pub. 1933) [Lloyd George was the Minister of Munitions and later, Prime Minister]**

❝ Glasgow was one of the worst districts, and the agitation amongst the workers seriously interfered with production, especially with the delivery of big guns. I decided to visit the works to see for myself what the position was, and to tell the men and their leaders the exact facts with regard to the military position, and the danger in which their fellow-workmen at the front were placed by the lack of adequate artillery.

I arrived at Glasgow on Christmas Eve, 1915 and went to Beardmore's works. In a loud challenging voice a man said 'I am as much a slave of Sir William Beardmore as if I had the letter "B" branded on my forehead'. This was my first meeting with Mr David Kirkwood.

TALKING POINT

Sources 4.3 and 4.4 give the opinions of a soldier in the trenches, the Minister of Munitions and a strike leader.

Discuss the reasons why they were for or against strikes in wartime.

What is your opinion?

Women War Workers

Before the War very few women went out to work. Those who did were usually unmarried and most worked as maids, cooks or cleaners for higher class people.

As the War took more and more male workers out of the factories and into the trenches, women began to take over men's jobs for the first time. The War gave women, who weren't yet allowed to vote, a chance to show that they were equal to men. They became conductors on trams and buses, munition workers and policewomen. Volunteers joined nurses working in hospitals. These volunteer nurses were called V.A.Ds. because they had joined the Volunteer Aid Detachment.

Other women helped in the Army and Navy by joining the newly formed Women's Army Auxiliary Corps (the W.A.A.C.) or the also new Women's Royal Naval Service (the W.R.N.S. or Wrens).

Everyone agreed that the women's effort was terrific. They certainly helped Britain to win the War.

Source 4.5
British war poster

THESE WOMEN ARE DOING THEIR BIT

LEARN TO MAKE MUNITIONS

Source 4.6

Mrs Cooper on the Gretna Munitions Works:

I went to Gretna in 1916. We lived in hostels, just wooden huts with long dormitories and a large living room with wooden forms to sit on and a big iron stove.

We worked in three shifts and we went to work in trains with wooden seats and each one of us had a pass to show before we were allowed in the large gates. We made cordite (an explosive). We changed into overalls and hats to cover our hair.

We made the cordite cut in lengths, packed it in trays and then carried it to small trucks at the doorway and two girls pushed the truck a mile [1.6 km] or so to large stoves where it was dried out. It was an awful job when on the trucks if you were on night shift – cold rain, dark and lonely pushing the heavy trucks and rats running round your feet. Sometimes the girls were drunk with fumes from the cordite and had to be taken to the sick bay (as we called it then) to sleep it off ... Dinner was always served cold but we ate it as we were always hungry.

We earned about £2 to £3 a week, with 13 shillings [65p] taken off for board and lodging.

Source 4.7

Women working in a Munitions Factory

Source 4.8

From the War Memoirs of David Lloyd George:

❝ The courage of the girls and women who worked in the shell-filling factories has never been properly recognised. They had to work under conditions of very real danger because they could lose their lives or injure themselves. There was also the fear of jaundice* from T.N.T. poisoning. [T.N.T. was another explosive material]. This turned their faces a bright repulsive yellow. For this reason the girls were nicknamed 'Canaries'.

For girls and women, who naturally prized their looks and complexion, the ugliness of T.N.T. poisoning was perhaps a peril even worse than the risk of explosion. ❞

40   * A disease of the liver which makes the skin go yellow.

Source 4.9

Women transport workers

Source 4.10

Ministry of Labour Poster

Hopkin's back and bandage it, paint and bandage Hibbert's foot, paint and bandage Hill's ankles and legs, put Johnson to bed and bandage him to his splint, and rub the chest of the man I always go to last thing at night.

It is delightful getting to know these people, which I never should if I had always remained Miss Brittain and never 'Nurse'. And I couldn't be treated more thoroughly as a nurse if I had been nursing for years. Of course the patients see little difference between a V.A.D. nurse and an ordinary hospital nurse.**"**

Source 4.11 _____

a) Vera Brittain as a V.A.D. nurse

b) Extract from Vera Brittain's War Diary, 1913–1917:

" _14 July 1915_: Eleven new patients suddenly arrived. We got through them somehow and of course as we were short-handed there was an unusually large number. Besides fetching basins, clearing away cups and filling hot water bottles, I had to rub a new patient's chest, rub

Source 4.12 _____

From the left, a W.A.A.C., a Wren and a Policewoman

Answer the following questions using the evidence provided by the sources.

1 Make a list of seven jobs which women could have taken up during the War to help the war effort.

2 What two things show that the women in source 4.5 were 'doing their bit' to win the War?

3 The following statements are all wrongly matched. Copy them, making the statements match correctly:

Women in the V.A.D. often	went yellow and were called canaries.
The W.A.A.C.s who wore a smart uniform	worked on the trams.
Women who worked in the munitions factories sometimes	worked as nurses.
Some women who were strong and smart	had duties in the Army.

4 Did Mrs Cooper (source 4.6) or Vera Brittain (source 4.11) find her war work more pleasant?
Give a reason for your answer.

5 Complete the sentences below. Source 4.10 will help you to fill the spaces.
The poster shows a woman who looks _____ and she is helping to provide soldiers with _____
The writing promises _____ wages, cheap _____ and cheap _____

6 How do you know that source 4.10 refers to a scheme run by the Government?

Treatment of Enemy Aliens

Germans living in Britain were called enemy *aliens*. People feared and hated them, although most were respectable citizens. They thought they might be spies!

Orders were made to send all Germans who weren't men of military age back to Germany. The men left were rounded up and put into prison camps.

These orders didn't apply to those Germans who were British citizens. They often changed their names to avoid being attacked by anti-German mobs. The same things happened to British citizens who lived in Germany.

Using source 4.13 discuss why German shopkeepers in Britain might need to make such quick changes. How would you feel if you were a German living in Britain at that time?

Source 4.13 _____

Cartoon from *Punch*, August 1914

A QUICK CHANGE OF FRONT.

Shortages in Britain and Germany

In 1914 there were about 45 million people living in Britain. Most of their food was brought in from overseas countries by ships called merchant ships. Germany tried to sink these ships by laying mines in the sea. She also built up a strong fleet of submarines or U-boats. These U-boats did great damage to Britain's merchant shipping by firing underwater *torpedoes*. At first only British ships were attacked but later all ships bringing supplies to Britain became targets for the U-boats.

The U-boat attacks had two effects on food in British shops – there were shortages and the prices went up. Rich people didn't mind very much because they could afford the high prices of food. But poor people often went hungry. By the end of 1917 things had got so bad that the Government rationed some essential foods. Everyone was given a ration book which had to be shown to shopkeepers when you bought rationed food. In this way the Food Controller made sure scarce food supplies were shared out fairly to everyone.

Britain used her navy to block Germany's ports and prevent important supplies

Source 4.14 _____

British War poster

Source 4.15 _____

British War poster

Source 4.16 _____

German War poster — *Aluminium, copper, brass, nickel, tin Hand it in, the army needs it*

Source 4.17 _____

German Iron Medal of 1916

In a hard time 1916   *I gave gold for defence*

I took iron for honour

getting through. So the Germans also had a shortage of food and rationing. Both nations had a shortage of metal to make munitions with and a shortage of money to pay for the war effort.

Source 4.18
Observer, **8 April 1917:**

❝ The usual week-end potato and coal scenes took place in London yesterday. The bread and potato queues were so long that the police had to keep them in order.

In South London trolleymen with coal were surrounded by people who had brought prams, wheelbarrows, go-carts and trucks, while others brought sacks, baskets and boxes to get their coal.

At Wrexham a big farm wagon full of potatoes was brought into the square. It was surrounded by hundreds of shouting people, most of them women, who scrambled on to the vehicle in their eagerness to buy. Several women fainted in the struggle, and the police were sent for to restore order. ❞

Source 4.19
From the Diary of the Rev. Andrew Clark:

❝ Saturday, 24 February 1917: 2.20 pm afternoon's post brought me a circular from the Food Controller asking all ministers of religion to encourage a voluntary reduction in the eating of food so that rationing wouldn't be necessary.

44

Thursday, 14 February, 1918: 9.40 am morning's post brought ration cards (a) butter and margarine; (b) butcher's meat, for each of the three members of this household. ❞

Source 4.20 a)
Ministry of Food Registration card dated 22 September, 1917

Source 4.20 b)
A German Bread Ration Book

Answer the following questions, using sources 4.14–20 to help you:

1 Why would British seamen want to give the message 'don't waste food'?
2 What did German women get in exchange for their gold and jewellery?
3 Which two statements below answer this question correctly? Why did German women feel it was worth giving up their gold?
   a) Because it gave help to Britain and France.
   b) Because it helped the German war effort.
   c) Because it bought medals for the brave German soldiers.
   d) Because it was the right thing to do.
4 Which source suggests that rationing was necessary in Britain?
   Give a reason for your answer.
5 Which *two* sources give evidence that Britain had food rationing in 1918?
6 Which of these two sources provides the more reliable evidence of the existence of food rationing? Give a reason for your answer.
7 Source 4.19 provides evidence that the Government didn't really want to bring in rationing. Was this because:
   a) it would mean a lot of extra work?
   b) it would be unfair?
   c) it would be against the wishes of rich people?
   d) it would cost too much?
   Copy what you think is the correct

reason and give an explanation for your choice.

German Raids on Civilians

During the War the Germans attacked British civilians from the sea and the air. About 1000 people were killed and others were injured or made homeless. For the first time in our history, bombs fell on people's houses. This was made possible by the invention of the airship by the German, Count von Zeppelin. Airships, called Zeppelins, were about 200 metres long (the length of a football pitch). They were enormous balloons filled with hydrogen gas. Below the balloon were two long cabins, called gondolas. One carried the crew and their bombs.

Later in the War bombing raids were made by German airplanes.

The attacks from the sea were made by German ships in the early days of the War. Their guns shelled towns on the east coast of England. The Royal Navy prevented any more raids of this type.

Source 4.21 _____

From Vera Brittain's War Diary:

❝ _16 Dec 1914:_ News arrived this morning of a raid by German ships on the East Coast. Scarborough, Whitby and Hartlepool have all been shelled. Some people say that 50 shells fell at Scarborough and it is reported that at Hartlepool nine persons were killed. **❞**

Source 4.22 _____

From the Diary of the Rev. A. Clark:

❝ _17 Oct 1914:_ Notice up at the Police Station opposite the Post Office that:
a) no lamps must show in shops;
b) as few lights as possible may show in the streets;
c) no lights must shine from windows of upper storeys;
d) no lobby-lights to be used unless shaded, so as not to show outside. **❞**

Source 4.23 _____

From Vera Brittain's War Diary:

❝ _10 Sept 1915:_ Rather a bad Zeppelin raid happened in London on Wednesday night. A new patient at the hospital told me that all the patients sat in their windows watching one of the Zeppelins. It looked like a great silver cigar in a cloud which was the smoke of the _shrapnel_ from our anti-aircraft guns bursting beneath it. One of the guns and the bombs

Source 4.24 _____

A Zeppelin

made a terrific noise. The hospital was in a turmoil all night from the patients with bad nerves. **❞**

WORK SECTION

Answer the following questions using sources 4.21–24 to help you:

1 Choose from the list five words which would best describe how you might feel if you were under attack from Zeppelins: PROUD, FRIGHTENED, PLEASED, SILLY, NERVOUS, HAPPY, DEPRESSED, WORRIED, ANGRY, BRAVE, DELIGHTED, GUILTY

2 Choose two methods from the following list to show that you know what the Government did to defend people against Zeppelin attacks:
a) Anti-aircraft guns were used.
b) Newspaper reports were censored.
c) Lighting restrictions were imposed.
d) Air-raid shelters were built.

WORD-FILE

Aliens People who have a different nationality from the people they live among.

Censorship The making of cuts in newspapers, films, letters, etc. to stop people reading or seeing something a person in authority doesn't want them to read or see. The person who makes the cuts is called a censor.

Civilians Ordinary members of the public who aren't soldiers, sailors or airmen.

Munitions Weapons, ammunition and equipment intended for military use.

Official Bulletin A short news statement put out by the Government or by someone in authority.

Propaganda A written statement, picture or film which tries to put a message across by deliberately exaggerating or distorting the facts.

Realm A country ruled by a king, a kingdom.

Shrapnel Small pieces of shell broken off as the shell explodes.

Strike The stopping of work usually by a group of workers organised by a Trade Union. It is used as a weapon to get better pay or conditions.

Torpedoes Cigar-shaped shells fired underwater from submarines.

 ACTIVITY

Make a picture of two Zeppelins dropping bombs. Put in a wrecked house, a dead body and an anti-aircraft gun.

Extension 1

The Defence of the Realm Act

This Extension will help you to learn more about DORA and its effects on the British people.

Once the Defence of the Realm Act had been passed, in August 1914, the Government was able to put out orders to control the civilian population without having to get the approval of Parliament.

This was a step towards giving the Government the powers of a dictator. Most people thought the extra power was necessary as the country was fighting a large-scale war. But many of the controls were irritating to people used to a great deal of freedom.

Source 4.25

Extract from the Defence of the Realm Act, 8 August 1914:

❝ An Act to confer on His Majesty in Council power to make Regulations during the present War for the Defence of the Realm.

Be it enacted by the King's most Excellent Majesty by and with the advice and consent of the Lords Spiritual and Temporal, and Commons, in this present

Parliament assembled, and by the authority of the same, as follows:

I. His Majesty in Council has power during the continuance of the present War to issue regulations as to the powers and duties of the Admiralty and Army Council, and of the members of His Majesty's forces, and other persons acting on His behalf, for securing the public safety and the defence of the realm; and by such regulations authorize the trial by courts martial and punishment of persons contravening any of the provisions of such regulations designed–

(a) to prevent persons communicating with the enemy or obtaining information for that purpose or any purpose calculated to jeopardize the success of the operations of any of His Majesty's forces or to assist the enemy... 99

▒▒▒▒ ASSIGNMENTS ▒▒▒▒

Use the source information and reference books where necessary.

1 Who was the King who 'enacted' the Defence of the Realm Act?
2 How long were the special powers given by DORA to the Government to last?
3 What are 'courts martial' and how are they different from ordinary courts in the way they deal with offenders?
4 Give three examples of controls on freedom which the Government ordered under the authority given by DORA. Why were such controls considered necessary?

CRAMPING HIS STYLE.

British Lion: "I'M GETTING A BIT TIRED OF THIS LADY. AFTER ALL, I AM A LION, AND NOT AN ASS."

Source 4.26 _____

Cartoon from *Punch* 9 April, 1919

5 Why has the cartoonist shown the Defence of the Realm Act as a dominating old woman sitting on a lion? Why were the British people 'a bit tired of this lady' by the end of the War?

Extension 2

The Changing Role of Women

This Extension will show you that the role of women changed out of all recognition because of the War. We shall look only at

British women, but the same changes happened to women in France, Germany and elsewhere.

As you have learned already very few women went out to work before the War. Those who did were usually unmarried professional women, like teachers, doctors and civil servants. Otherwise they were working-class women who worked in middle- and upper-class houses. And no woman, however rich or clever, was allowed to vote or be a Member of Parliament.

Before the War a Women's Rights Movement worked hard to improve the lot of women. Its great success was the acceptance of women doctors. The most famous Women's-Rights campaign was that of the Suffragettes but by 1914 they had made no progress in securing votes for women.

After the outbreak of War Emmeline Pankhurst and her Suffragettes took the lead in taking up work in every kind of man's job. They also joined the various 'Women's Armies'. By doing so they showed they had earned the right to be equal with men.

The contribution of the women of Britain to the war effort was enormous. Their reward came in 1918 when the all-male Parliament granted the vote to women over 30.

Source 4.27 _____

From the War Memoirs of D. Lloyd George:

66 On 18th July, 1915, they headed a

great Women's War Pageant, in which thousands of women demonstrators marched for miles along London streets through rain and mud, escorting a deputation that waited on me, as Minister of Munitions, to express their welcome of the National Register, and to offer their services to help the country. While voicing the demand of the women to be permitted to take part in war work Mrs. Pankhurst also put in a plea for wage conditions which would safeguard their standard of living and prevent them from being sweated or exploited by manufacturers. **"**

Source 4.28

Cartoon from *Punch* August 1916

THE WAR WORKERS.

"WHAT'S ALL THIS CACKLE ABOUT VOTES AND A NEW REGISTER?"
"DON'T KNOW—OR CARE. WE'RE ALL TOO BUSY JUST NOW."

Source 4.29

From How We Lived Then 1914–1918 **by Mrs C. S. Peel:**

" From 1917 onwards the Women's Armies were a great feature of war life. The first of the armies was the Land Army, then followed the W.R.N.S. (Women's Royal Naval Service), with their punning motto 'Never at Sea'. The original staff were chiefly composed of V.A.D.'s... The Navy, a very conservative service, was somewhat startled by the idea of a woman's section, for 'Wrens', as they were nicknamed, not only filled the posts of cooks, waitresses and housemaids, but were also employed in important confidential work. This occasioned some alarm amongst officers, who feared that they would give away secret information, a fear which, as far as is publicly known, did not materialize into a fact. **"**

▓▓▓ ASSIGNMENTS ▓▓▓

Use the source information and reference books where necessary.
(Note: The National Register was introduced by the Government to help them solve the problem of shortage of labour. Everyone, between 15 and 65, was compelled to give details of age and occupation.)

1 How would the National Register help the Government to cope with the labour shortage? Why would women 'express their welcome of the National Register' to Lloyd George (source 4.27)?

2 In source 4.28 what is the man making and what is the woman carrying? What industry are they working in together?

3 Is the cartoonist (source 4.28) for or against the employment of women in wartime? Give a reason for your answer.

4 'We're all too busy just now' (source 4.28). Make a list of five other types of work undertaken by women during the War. Don't include the armed services.

5 What do the letters V.A.D. stand for? What kind of work did the women in the V.A.D. do?

6 Find out the names of the three 'Women's Armies' (only two are mentioned in source 4.29). What are the two meanings of 'Never at Sea' which make it such a good motto for one of these 'Women's Armies'?

7 'They would give away secret information' (source 4.29). What other fears about women doing so-called men's work proved to be false?

8 The poster in source 4.30 shows two graphs. What do the two graphs tell us about the *actual number* of women employed compared with the number of women in Government jobs? What do the two graphs tell us about the *rise* in numbers employed? Account for the steeper rise after 1915.

9 Write a speech to support the opinion that by 1917 British women had earned the right to vote.

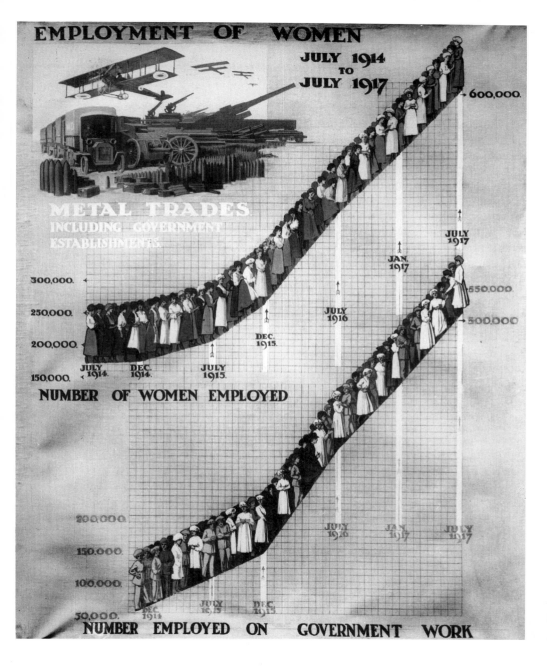

Source 4.30 _____

A Government poster

5 The End of the War

The World at War

You have been learning about the fighting on the Western Front where the Germans were up against the British and French. There were other fronts in other parts of the world and many other nations joined in the fighting.

There was fighting between the Turks (allies of Germany) and the British in Palestine and in Turkey itself. There was the Eastern Front where Germans and Austrians fought the Russians (allies of Britain and France). In northern Italy, Italians and Austrians fought each other.

Britain, France and Germany all owned land in Africa. So there was fighting in Africa over the ownership of this land. Japan declared war on Germany in 1914 and was soon attacking German ships in the Pacific Ocean. She also attacked German-owned land in China.

In April 1917, the United States of America declared war on Germany. The name of the American President was Woodrow Wilson. He had hoped to keep America neutral. But two things happened which made the Americans very angry with the Germans.
1 In 1915 a German U-boat sank the great British passenger ship, *Lusitania*. There were 128 Americans on board. They were all drowned.
2 Early in 1917 the Germans decided to order their U-boats to sink all ships sailing to Britain and France. This included ships belonging to neutral nations like America.

President Wilson declared war on Germany and American soldiers soon joined the British and French on the Western Front. The American soldiers were called 'doughboys'. They were tough and very keen to have a go at the Germans.

But in November 1917 came bad news for the allies. A revolution in Russia brought Lenin and the *Bolsheviks* into power. Russia became the first Communist nation. Lenin made peace with Germany

---

WHAT YOU WILL LEARN

Unit 5 will help you to understand:
1 Why the U.S.A. decided to enter the War.
2 Why the Germans were defeated after a last 'Big Push'.
3 The terrible effects of the First World War on nations and on the lives of ordinary people.
4 How the War changed the power and influence of nations in relation to each other.
5 The immense power and influence of President Wilson.
6 What the peace settlement made after the War was like.

Source 5.1
U.S.A. Government poster

Source 5.2
President Wilson's speech to Congress (the American Parliament):

   ❝ Vessels of every kind, whatever their flag, their cargo, their destination, their errand, have been ruthlessly sent to the bottom without warning or thought of help – the vessels of friendly neutrals, even hospital ships.

> The present German warfare is a warfare against mankind. The world must be made safe for *democracy*. **"**

Source 5.3

U.S.A. Government poster

ONLY THE NAVY CAN STOP THIS

WORK SECTION

Answer the following questions, using sources 5.1–3 to help you.

1 In President Wilson's speech, which of the following groups of words show that Wilson was trying to work up strong feelings against Germany?

their cargo
ruthlessly sent
without warning
present German warfare
warfare against mankind

2 According to Wilson, the defeat of Germany would make the world 'safe for democracy'.
Does this mean:
a) All Germany's lands in Africa would be free?
b) Free nations like France would no longer be threatened by Germany?
c) Germany would free herself from rule by the Kaiser?
d) Germany would stop sinking neutral ships?
Copy the *one* correct answer.

3 The poster in source 5.3 explains the main reason why America entered the War.
Was this reason:
a) to stop Germany bombing American cities?
b) to stop Germany invading America?
c) to stop Germany sinking neutral ships?
d) to stop Germany killing innocent children?
Copy the *one* correct answer.

4 The poster in source 5.3 is propaganda because it exaggerates the true situation. Which four items out of the following list help to exaggerate the true situation:
the German helmet?
the pirate's scarf round the helmet?
the bloody sword?
the rolled up sleeves?
the belt?
the crossed bones at the neck?
the drowning of children?

The German 'Big Push, 1918

In March, 1918, the Germans decided to start a huge attack on the Western Front. They hoped this time to break through the British and French front line and go on to win the War.

The time was right for two reasons: Firstly, with Russia out of the War Germany could move the Army, which had been fighting the Russians, across to the Western Front.
Secondly, the biggest flood of fresh American 'doughboys' had not yet arrived on the Western Front.

Just for a few months in 1918 Germany felt she had a chance to win. The Germans advanced in many places on the front but were stopped at the second Battle of the Marne in July.

The Defeat of Germany

Then the tide turned against Germany. By now the Americans were arriving in great numbers. The allies had a big lead in tanks and aircraft. Also the naval blockade of the German ports was causing great hardship to German civilians. Their shops were empty of goods of all kinds including food and clothing.

The British and French began a huge attack on 8 August 1918. Slowly but surely the Germans were driven out of France (see map). In Germany people rose up against the Kaiser. He had to give up his throne and Germany became a republic.

At 11 am on 11 November 1918, the two sides agreed to an *armistice* which brought the fighting to an end. The First World War was over.

Source 5.4

Special Order of the Day by Field Marshal Sir Douglas Haig

SPECIAL ORDER OF THE DAY
By FIELD-MARSHAL SIR DOUGLAS HAIG
K.T., G.C.B., G.C.V.O., K.C.I.E
Commander-in-Chief, British Armies in France.

To ALL RANKS OF THE BRITISH ARMY IN FRANCE AND FLANDERS.

Three weeks to-day the enemy began his terrific attacks against us on a fifty-mile front. His objects are to separate us from the French, to take the Channel Ports and destroy the British Army.

In spite of throwing already 106 Divisions into the battle and enduring the most reckless sacrifice of human life, he has as yet made little progress towards his goals.

We owe this to the determined fighting and self-sacrifice of our troops. Words fail me to express the admiration which I feel for the splendid resistance offered by all ranks of our Army under the most trying circumstances.

Many amongst us now are tired. To those I would say that Victory will belong to the side which holds out the longest. The French Army is moving rapidly and in great force to our support.

There is no other course open to us but to fight it out. Every position must be held to the last man: there must be no retirement. With our backs to the wall and believing in the justice of our cause each one of us must fight on to the end. The safety of our homes and the Freedom of mankind alike depend upon the conduct of each of us at this critical moment.

General Headquarters,
Thursday, April 11th, 1918.

*Commander-in-Chief,
British Armies in France.*

PRINTED IN FRANCE BY ARMY PRINTING AND STATIONERY SERVICES.   PRESS A—4/18.

ACTIVITY

Work together in five groups to turn the map below into a large wall map. Each group makes one of the following:
a) coastline and rivers;
b) international boundaries;
c) place names, scale and compass;
d) all lines showing position of armies;
e) area of regained terrirtory and arrows.
   Then each group makes a paper flag for

one nation – Belgium, Britain, France, America and Germany to pin on the map.

Source 5.5

My War Memories by General Ludendorff (pub. 1919):

“ August 8th was the black day of the German Army in this war. The British and the French attacked with strong squadrons of tanks early on August 8th,

The Western Front in 1918

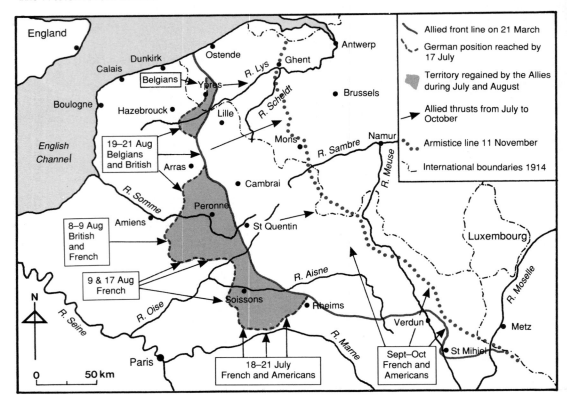

in a dense fog, made still thicker by artificial smoke.

They penetrated deep into our positions . . . some of our *divisions* allowed themselves to be completely overwhelmed.

On the other hand the losses of the enemy had been extraordinarily small. The balance of numbers had moved heavily against us. It was bound to become increasingly unfavourable as more American troops moved in.

Reports came in of behaviour I should not have thought possible in the German Army. Whole groups of our men had surrendered to single troopers or isolated squadrons. Retiring troops, meeting a fresh division going bravely into action, had shouted out things like *'Black-Leg'* and 'You're making the war last longer than it need'. The officers in many places lost their control. **"**

WORK SECTION

Answer the following questions using sources 5.4 and 5.5 to help you.

1 According to Haig, what were the three aims of the German 'Big Push' in April 1918?

2 Do Haig's words 'With our backs to the wall' mean that the British Army was either:
   a) being very hard pressed by the Germans?

or
   b) going to attack the Germans from the back?
   Copy the correct answer.

3 Write down four reasons why, from 8 August 1918, the Germans began to lose the War.

The Effects of the War

Sources 5.6–10 which follow allow you to work out the terrible effects of the First World War on all nations that took part.

The victorious nations as well as the defeated nations were badly hit by the War.

Sources 5.11–12 look at the effects of the War on two individuals who fought in the War. One is German and the other is British.

The First World War cost more than any other war in history if you add together casualties, money spent and general destruction.

Source 5.6

Casualties

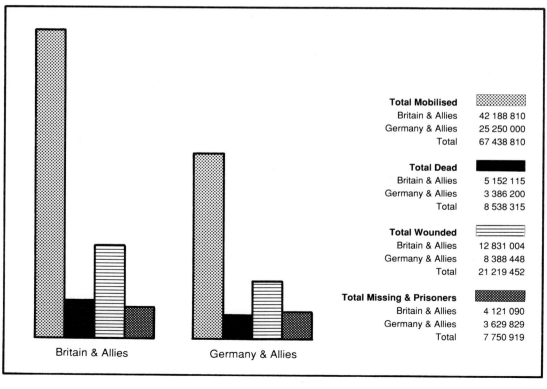

Total Mobilised		
Britain & Allies	42 188 810	
Germany & Allies	25 250 000	
Total	67 438 810	
Total Dead		
Britain & Allies	5 152 115	
Germany & Allies	3 386 200	
Total	8 538 315	
Total Wounded		
Britain & Allies	12 831 004	
Germany & Allies	8 388 448	
Total	21 219 452	
Total Missing & Prisoners		
Britain & Allies	4 121 090	
Germany & Allies	3 629 829	
Total	7 750 919	

Britain & Allies   Germany & Allies

Source 5.7

Grave of the Unknown Soldier (above)
Westminster Abbey and the Cenotaph,
Whitehall, London (right)

Source 5.8 a)

Verse of a War Poem by Lt.-Col. John McRae:

> In Flanders fields the poppies blow
> Between the crosses, row on row
> That mark our place, and in the sky
> The larks, still bravely singing, fly
> Scarce heard amid the groans
> below.

Source 5.8 b)

A Remembrance Poppy

Source 5.8 c)

A British War Cemetery in France

Money

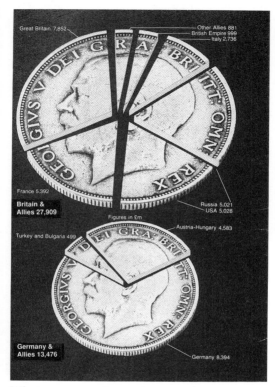

What governments spent

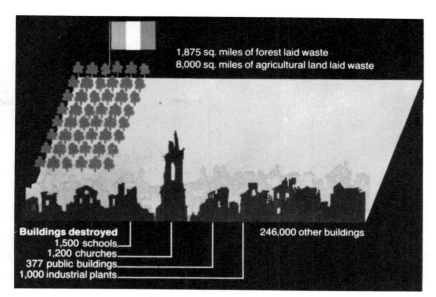

1,875 sq. miles of forest laid waste
8,000 sq. miles of agricultural land laid waste

Buildings destroyed
1,500 schools
1,200 churches
377 public buildings
1,000 industrial plants

246,000 other buildings

Source 5.10

Loss of land and buildings in France

WORK SECTION

Answer the following questions, using sources 5.6–5.10 to help you.

1 Which nation suffered the greatest number of casualties – was it Russia, Germany or Britain?

2 Give a reason why America had such a small number of casualties?

3 Which side came off worse in numbers of casualties – was it Germany and her allies or Britain and her allies?

4 In what three ways do the sources show how Britain remembers the dead of the First World War?

5 Why was the poppy chosen by the Haig Fund as the badge of remembrance?

6 Write *true* or *false* against each of the following statements:
   a) The War cost Britain more than any of her allies.
   b) The War cost Germany more than any of her allies.
   c) The War cost Germany and her allies more than it cost Britain and her allies.

7 Why did France suffer greater destruction of land and buildings than any other nation fighting the War?

8 Which nation had the best reason for wanting revenge against Germany – was it Britain, Italy, America or France? Give a reason for your answer.

Source 5.11

From the Diary of Seaman Richard Stumpf, German Navy:

❝ *11 November 1918*: No pen in the world could possibly describe my emotions these past three days. I looked on with grief as our fleet was hurriedly prepared for surrender.

17 November 1918: Although we have now been free for ten days, we are still not happy. Worries about the future make our spirits low. Very few of us have regular or well-paying trades.

18 November 1918: Today is a very sad day for me. At this moment the ships are assembling for their final voyage. The submarines will also be going. It is like a funeral. We shall not see them again. [The German Navy sailed to Scapa Flow in Orkney. There they were *scuttled* (sunk) by their German crews]. I wish I had not been born a German. . . . I shall be discharged from the navy in another few days. But I had always seen it entirely differently. There will be no flowers, no wreaths, no tolling bells and no merry receptions.

My *Fatherland*, My dear *Fatherland*, what will happen to you now? **"**

Source 5.12

With a Machine Gun to Cambrai by **George Coppard**:

" Lloyd George and company had been full of big talk about making a country fit for heroes to live in, but it was just so much hot air. No practical steps were taken to help the broad mass of *demobbed* men, and I joined the queues for jobs as messengers, window cleaners and dish washers. It was a complete let-down for thousands like me, and for some young officers too. It was a common sight in London to see ex-officers with barrel organs, trying to earn a living as beggars – the Government never kept their promise.

During this time the Government was trying to fix the enormous sums to be given as presents to the high-ranking officers who had won the War for them. Field Marshal Sir Douglas Haig and Admiral Sir David Beatty received a tax-free golden hand-shake* of £100 000 (a colossal sum then) and an earldom for doing the jobs they were paid to do. . . . If any reader should ask 'What did the demobbed Tommy think about all this?' I can only say! 'Well, what do *you* think'? **"**

* Golden hand-shake: a very large sum of money given as a farewell present to an employee.

TALKING POINT

Read sources 5.11 and 5.12 carefully. Then divide into two groups, Germans and British. Discuss in your groups how you would feel if you were a demobbed serviceman in 1918. Then come together as a class to see how your feelings are the same and how they are different.

Position of the Great Powers, 1918

In Unit 1 you learned that some nations are more powerful than others. The most powerful are called Great Powers. They could influence weak nations and make them obey.

Before the War Britain was the most powerful nation in the world. After the War the United States of America took over this position from Britain.

France and Italy were still considered as Great Powers. Both had been on the victorious side in the War. But France's sacrifices had been greater and she stood equal to Britain in the eyes of the world. The 'Big Four', as they were called, and their leaders stood in a league table like this:

No. 1
United States of America
led by President Wilson

No. 2
Great Britain led by
D. Lloyd George,
Prime Minister

No. 2
France led by
G. Clemenceau,
Prime Minister

No. 4
Italy led by Orlando,
Prime Minister

The defeated nations, Germany, Austria-Hungary and Turkey, had lost their position as Great Powers completely.

So the First World War made a big change to the international power situation.

Source 5.13

Cartoon of Woodrow Wilson by Owen Wood

How Should Germany be Treated?

Everyone hoped for lasting peace after the horrors of the World War. This had to be made 'the war to end war', as many people said. President Wilson got in first with his ideas for a settlement. These ideas were called 'The Fourteen Points'. He was keen to see that Germany was treated fairly. It would not be sensible to punish her too severely.

Britain and France were more concerned with making Germany pay for the War. If Germany's wealth and power were stripped away, she would be too weak to go to war again. In addition, the French wanted to become safer by getting a more easily defended frontier with Germany. The French leader Clemenceau, was nick-named 'The Tiger'.

Source 5.14

Comments by Harold Nicolson, a British diplomat:

❝ The President had come to Paris armed with more power than any man in history had possessed. He had come fired with high ideals . . . and Paris saw in him a rather comic and very irritating professor.❞

Source 5.15

Extract from a speech by Sir E. Geddes:

❝ I have personally no doubt we will get everything out of Germany that you can squeeze out of a lemon and a bit more... I suggest that not only all the gold Germany has got, but all the silver and jewels she has got, shall be handed over... I would strip Germany as she has stripped Belgium.❞

Source 5.16

Extracts from the Army Diary of Col. R. Meinertzhagen:

❝ [Here he refers to public opinion in Britain:]

8th May 1919: The newspapers and public opinion at home claim the enforcement of the most severe punishment upon the defeated enemy.

[But his own views were different:] The British Empire is in a very fine position at the present moment, and we now need a peace which will keep us in that position. If we are too greedy and revengeful our advantages will disappear.❞

WORK SECTION

Use sources 5.13–16 to help you answer the following questions:

1 Does Owen Wood's picture of Wilson in source 5.13 agree with the comments of Harold Nicolson in source 5.14? Yes or No? Give a reason for your answer.

2 How does the cartoonist show Wilson being
   a) 'armed with power'?
   b) 'comic'?
   c) 'irritating'?
   Select your answers to a), b) and c) from the following list – wearing gloves for cutting; making his own shapes out of Europe's nations; handling a huge pair of scissors.

3 What evidence can you find in either source 5.15 or source 5.16 to show that:
   a) Many people in Britain wanted to make Germany suffer for causing the War?
   b) Not all British people shared this view?

The Peace Settlement

The Peace Conference was held at Versailles, near Paris, in 1919. *Representatives* of all the victorious nations were present. But the leaders of the 'Big Four' controlled everything. They used their influence to make the others agree with them.

President Wilson had the most influence. But he had to give way to Clemenceau and Lloyd George on some points.

Once all the decisions affecting Germany had been made, they were written into a document called the Treaty of Versailles. Everyone then assembled in the Hall of Mirrors in the Palace of Versailles. The two representatives of Germany were called in, like prisoners entering a court room. They were shown where to sign the Treaty and did so. Representatives from all the other nations then signed in turn.

You can find out about the most important terms of the Treaty of Versailles by looking at source 5.17 a), b) and c).

Source 5.17

a) The new map of Germany

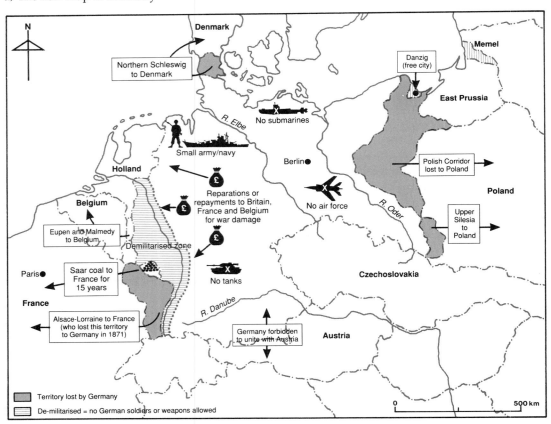

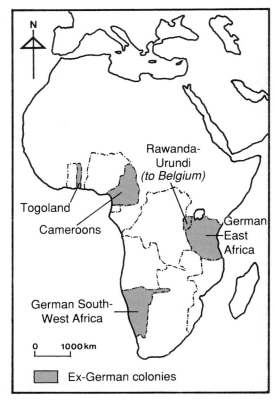

b) Colonies taken away from Germany

WANTED DEAD OR ALIVE!

GUILT CLAUSE

Germany must admit that she and her allies were to blame for causing the War. Also all the losses and damage in the War were the fault of Germany and her allies.

c)

Source 5.18

Extract from the German newspaper Deutsche Zeitung **28 June 1919:**

“ Vengeance!

German nation!

Today in the Hall of Mirrors at Versailles a disgraceful treaty is being signed. Never forget it! On the spot where, in the glorious year of 1871, the German Empire in all its glory began, today German honour is dragged to the grave. Never forget it! The German people, with unceasing labour, will push forward to reconquer that place among the nations of the world to which they are entitled. There will be vengeance for the shame of 1919. ”

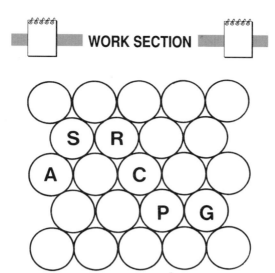

1 Use source 5.17 a), b) and c) to help you answer the questions correctly.
What A was the land given back to France?
What S was the coal area to be used by France for 15 years?
What R was the German territory to be de-militarised?
What C were the lands outside Europe taken from Germany?
What P was land lost by Germany to Poland?
What G was the part of the Treaty which blamed Germany for the War?

2 Use source 5.18 to help you answer these questions. The newspaper extract was printed on the day the Treaty of Versailles was signed. It was printed on the front page with a black mourning band around it.
a) Did the German people think the Treaty of Versailles was fair or unfair? Give reasons for your answer.
b) The newspaper is trying to get its readers to be angry about the Treaty by:
calling on people to take revenge;
appealing to the pride of the Germans;
telling people to bear with things for a while;
going into mourning for German honour.
Which three of these statements are correct?

The Settlement with Germany's Allies

Other peace treaties were signed which dealt with Austria-Hungary and Turkey.

In his 'Fourteen Points' Wilson had said that nations had the right to govern themselves. You will remember that the Emperor of Austria-Hungary ruled over many nations. After the War these nations demanded independence and their demands were granted by the victorious allies.

The Austro-Hungarian Empire was broken up into many small countries. Austria itself was left as a tiny German-speaking nation. But it was not allowed to unite with Germany. Some of the nations were too small or weak to be made into separate countries. So Yugoslavia and Czechoslovakia were created to contain several nations. The map in source 5.19 shows the carve-up of Austria-Hungary after the War.

Source 5.19

End of the Austro-Hungarian Empire

Germany
0   500 km
N
Poland
Galicia
Czechoslovakia
Switzerland
Austria
Tyrol
Hungary
Transylvania
Trieste
Rumania
Fiume
Croatia
Dalmatia
Bosnia
Yugoslavia
Bulgaria
Italy
Albania
Mediterranean
Sea

〜〜〜 Frontier of Austria-
Hungary 1914

–·–·– National frontiers 1919

The Turkish Empire was also carved up. The nations which had been ruled by Turkey didn't get their independence. Instead they were to be ruled either by Britain or France.

WORD-FILE

Armistice   An agreement by both sides in a war to stop the fighting.

Black-leg   A traitor to fellow-workers such as someone who works while fellow-workers are on strike. Someone who sucks up to authority.

Bolsheviks   The name of the Russian Communist Party.

Demobbed   Released from the armed services into civilian life. This process is called demobilisation or demobbing.

Division   A very large section of an Army. In Britain a Division is commanded by a Major-General.

Democracy   A nation, like Britain, France and the U.S.A., which elects its own government and whose people have a large amount of freedom.

Fatherland   An affectionate word used by Germans for the country where they were born – Germany.

Representatives   People who do a job on behalf of a society or nation. They often present views at conferences. M.Ps in Britain represent the people who elected them.

Extension 1

The Defeat of Germany

This Extension will help you to evaluate in detail the reasons for the defeat of Germany in 1918.

Source 5.20

Extracts from the War Memoirs of D. Lloyd George:

" The knowledge was slowly sinking through all ranks of the German Army that the War was lost. For four years they had believed themselves to be certain of victory and as recently as midsummer of 1918 they had been promised a final victory.

The German Army was melting away, while the Allies were being reinforced by the steadily rising flood of American troops. The new German recruits were a source of weakness rather than of strength for they had been dragged unwillingly from safe, well-paid work in munitions factories and many of them were filled with Bolshevik ideas. Whenever possible they went sick. At the first opportunity they ran away.

In Germany most of the population were suffering hardship as the result of the blockade.

In another important respect the Entente had a great superiority to aid their march to victory. This was the tank. The Germans surprisingly neglected to develop the new device. The tactics of the massed tank attack were adopted by the allies repeatedly in 1918.

In the summer and autumn of 1918 Haig was fulfilling a role for which he was admirably adapted, that of second in command to a general of unchallenged genius, Foch [the French Field-Marshal] who was responsible for the general plan of attack on the whole front.

The allies had 5646 aeroplanes; the Germans 4000. By Sept. 1918 all the allies of Germany were beaten. On the battlefield the allied troops pressed forward with a new confidence, born of the certainty that they were now superior in men, material and leadership. "

ASSIGNMENTS

Use the source information and reference books, where necessary.

1 What happened before midsummer, 1918, which would have made German soldiers believe that the promise of final victory was coming true?
2 Why, according to Lloyd George, was the German Army 'melting away'?
3 'Bolshevik ideas'. What nation had recently turned Bolshevik? Who now led that nation? What party would you probably belong to if you had Bolshevik ideas?
4 What was 'the blockade' which was causing hardship to German civilians and what kind of hardships were they suffering?
5 Copy words from source 5.20 which show that Lloyd George had a poor opinion of Haig as a military leader.
6 Explain how the Allies by September of 1918 were 'superior in men, material and leadership'.

Extension 2

The Treaty of Versailles

This Extension will reinforce and extend your knowledge of the peace settlement with Germany.

Source 5.21

Speech by D. Lloyd George in the House of Commons on 3 July 1919:

" The last time I had the opportunity of addressing the House upon this Treaty I ventured to call it a 'stern, but a just Treaty'. I stick to that description. The terms are in many respects terrible terms to impose upon a country. What do these terms mean to Germany?

In 1914 she had an Empire which possessed the greatest army in the world. It was the terror of the world. It has now been reduced to the size of a force quite adequate to maintain the peace in

Germany, but not equal to disturbing the peace of the feeblest of her neighbours.

There was a navy, the second in the world. Where is it now?

The colonies of Germany covered about 1 500 000 square miles. Stripped of the lot! Territories of the size and of the wealth of, say, Scotland and Wales, torn from her side.

The ruler who for thirty years spoke for Germany's pride and her majesty and her might is soon to be placed on his trial.

They are terrible terms. Her war debt is more than doubled in order to pay reparations. There is no doubt that the terms are stern. Are they just?

Take the territorial terms. In so far as territories have been taken away from Germany, it is a restoration – they are all territories that ought not to belong to Germany, and they are now restored to their independence.**"**

Source 5.22

Punch cartoon, 11 Dec. 1918

WANTED.

WILLIAM THE GALLANT (*to Holland*). "COURAGE! I WILL NEVER DESERT YOU."

▬▬▬ **ASSIGNMENTS** ▬▬▬

Use the source information and reference books where necessary.

1 Describe how 'the greatest army in the world' was reduced and restricted in its operation by the Treaty of Versailles.
2 'Where is it now?' What happened to the German navy in 1919?
3 What does Lloyd George mean by 'to pay reparations'? Why do you think Germany found it impossible to make payments to the Allies?
4 Why was the Kaiser not, in fact, 'placed on his trial'?
5 Why does Lloyd George say that territories taken away from Germany by the Treaty of Versailles 'ought not to belong to Germany'?
6 Make a list of all the territories taken from Germany by the Treaty. Choose two and explain how it was 'a restoration'.

6 The League of Nations

Wilson's Great Idea

President Wilson's greatest idea for stopping wars had nothing to do with punishing Germany. He believed that a club should be started for all the nations of the world to join. This club would be able to discuss a quarrel or disagreement between the member nations. It would then work out a settlement. In this way the world would be safe from wars. Then everyone would have *security* and feel that peace would last.

You learned in Unit 1 that nations were like people. When people quarrel they often end up fighting. But a fight can sometimes be prevented if the causes of the quarrel are talked over with someone else. This was how Wilson thought his international club would work.

Wilson first put forward his great idea in the 'Fourteen Points' written before the War was over. The idea was accepted by the Allies. Even before the club was started a name had been found for it – the League of Nations.

Wilson's Triumphant Tour

In December 1918, President Wilson set out from the White House in Washington to visit Europe. His tour took him first to Paris, then to London and Rome. Then he returned to Paris to attend the Peace Conference.

Wilson was greeted everywhere as a hero. Vast crowds cheered and waved American flags. Here was the man who could stop wars happening again! In Italy there were signs saying 'Long live Wilson, God of Peace'. In his speeches Wilson spoke of his hopes for a League of Nations. There was no doubt in his mind that the people of France, Britain and Italy all agreed with him.

At the Peace Conference in Paris there was also agreement about the League of Nations. The decision to set up the League of Nations was part of the Treaty of Versailles.

WHAT YOU WILL LEARN

Unit 6 will help you to understand:
1 The aims of the League of Nations.
2 The part President Wilson played in setting up the League.
3 The attitudes of Britain, France and America to the League.
4 How the League was organised.
5 How the League tried to improve conditions of people all over the world.
6 Why the League was too weak to protect the world from wars.

Source 6.1

Extract from the Daily Express, **27 December 1918:**

“ WONDERFUL WELCOME TO PRESIDENT WILSON TRIUMPHAL PROGRESS THROUGH ENORMOUS CROWDS

President Wilson received a magnificent welcome from London. It marked the proudest and happiest moments in the relations between the two great English-speaking democracies.

'I am deeply touched', was the President's simple acknowledgement of his reception.

The special train arrived just on time and a moment later the King and President Wilson were shaking hands…

While the band played 'The Star-Spangled Banner', the President stood erect, silk hat in hand, and the King stood at the salute…

President Wilson looked like the Rock of Gibraltar…**”**

Source 6.2

A woman's letter to a French newspaper:

“ Wilson, you have given back the father to his home, the ploughman to his field. You have saved our fiancés. Love blooms again. Wilson, you have saved our children. Through you evil is punished. Wilson! Wilson! Glory to you, who like Jesus has said 'Peace on Earth and Goodwill to Men'.**”**

Source 6.3

President Wilson and Mrs Wilson during their European tour

WORK SECTION

Use sources 6.1–3 to help you answer the following questions:

1 Why was Wilson given such a magnificent welcome by the people of Britain, France and Italy in 1918? Answer by copying the two correct answers from the list below:

a) People thought he would make a lasting peace in the world.

b) People could understand him because he spoke English.

c) People believed his country had helped to defeat the Germans.

d) People liked cheering presidents more than cheering kings.

2 What evidence can you find in source 6.1 to show what President Wilson thought about his welcome in Britain?

3 Source 6.2 is a French woman's letter which exaggerates Wilson's importance. What words show that the woman thinks he is almost like God?

What Americans thought about the League

The League of Nations was now part of the Treaty of Versailles which President Wilson had signed. But the U.S.A. could only take part in the League if the *Congress* (American Parliament) agreed. Wilson had many enemies in the Congress who thought America should have nothing to do with the problems of other nations.

They had given enough help by joining the War. Now they felt Americans should just get on with the job of making America even richer than it was already. This task wouldn't be helped by getting mixed up in the problems of other nations.

Wilson believed that acceptance of the League was the only way to preserve peace. He said that American soldiers would have died for nothing unless the U.S.A. played her part in the League of Nations. He tried hard to get people to agree by making many speeches.

But when the Congress voted, the enemies of Wilson won. The Congress decided by only seven votes to refuse to accept the Treaty of Versailles. This meant that the U.S.A. also refused to join the League of Nations.

President Wilson ended his presidency in disappointment and failure.

What the French and British thought about the League

France and Britain were the most important supporters of the League of Nations once the U.S.A. had refused to join. They had very different views about the League. *The French View:* France felt that Britain had too much influence in the League. This was because the nations of the British Empire like Canada and Australia had a vote in the Assembly of the League as well as Britain. In those days the Empire Nations usually did what Britain said. So France said Britain had more than one vote!

Also the first Secretary-General of the League was British.

France wanted to use the League to make sure Germany didn't rise up again. She thought the League should have more power to make member nations obey the rules.

The British View: Britain didn't like the idea of using force against member nations who disobeyed the rules. In spite of this the British Government firmly supported the

League. Many British people joined the League of Nations Association. The Association held meetings and rallies. It also raised money to support the work of the League.

Source 6.4

Punch cartoon, Dec. 1919

THE GAP IN THE BRIDGE.

Source 6.5

A League of Nations rally in Hyde Park, London June, 1921

WORK SECTION

Use sources 6.4 and 6.5 to help you answer the following questions.

The cartoon in source 6.4 shows the attitude of the American people to the League of Nations:

1 Name the cartoon character who stands for the U.S.A.
2 Which of these words describes the attitude of the U.S.A. to the League best: hopeful, pleased, couldn't-care-less, thinking it over?
Give a reason for your choice.
3 How does the artist show that the U.S.A. is very important for the success of the League?
4 What in the cartoon suggests that President Wilson expected that the U.S.A. would join?
5 Which of the four stones of the bridge is incorrectly named? What is the correct name?

The photograph in source 6.5 shows that some people in Britain gave support to the League of Nations:

1 What kind of people are shown at the Hyde Park rally? Are they: young/elderly, working class/middle class, well-dressed/ badly dressed?
Copy the correct three answers.
2 Does the photograph in source 6.5 prove that the kind of people shown were the *only* kind of people in Britain who supported the League? Give a reason for your answer.
3 How does the photograph in source 6.5 tell us that some people in Britain were strongly in support of the League?

ACTIVITY

The League of Nations didn't have a flag of its own unlike the present-day United Nations which does. Design a flag of your own for the League.

How the League was Organised

The Headquarters: It was agreed that Geneva in Switzerland should be the home of the League. In the early years hotels and other buildings housed the League. Between 1929 and 1936 a permanent Palace of the League of Nations was built on the shores of Lake Geneva. Many of the member nations shared the building work. If you go there today you will see marble from one country, wood from another and so on.

The Assembly of the League: This was a kind of parliament for representatives of all the member nations. All member nations had one vote each. It meet at regular intervals.

The Council of the League: This was a kind of government for the League. It was provided by permanent members (Britain, France, Italy, Japan and, later, Germany) and a small number of temporary members elected for three years by the members of the Assembly. It could meet at any time to take quick action in emergencies.

The Secretariat of the League: This was a kind of *civil service*. Like ordinary governments, the Council of the League could not do its work without the help of paid permanent officials or civil servants. The Secretariat recruited officials from any of its member nations. They did all the office work, prepared reports and kept records.

The International Court of Justice: The Court was made up of judges from member nations. Member nations could submit their disagreement to the Court. The judges would then decide their ruling. The Court also had the power to say what treaties or other international agreements really meant.

The International Court was the only part of the League which didn't meet in Geneva. Its courthouse was in The Hague, a city in the Netherlands.

The International Labour Organisation: This organisation was called the I.L.O for short. It had the task of improving conditions for workers all over the world.

Source 6.6

Message from the Government of Switzerland, March 1919:

“ Switzerland would consider it a great honour to offer the hospitality of its territory should the League of Nations wish to establish its headquarters there. **”**

Source 6.7

Architect's model of the League of Nations in Geneva

Source 6.8

Map of the world showing League membership in 1920

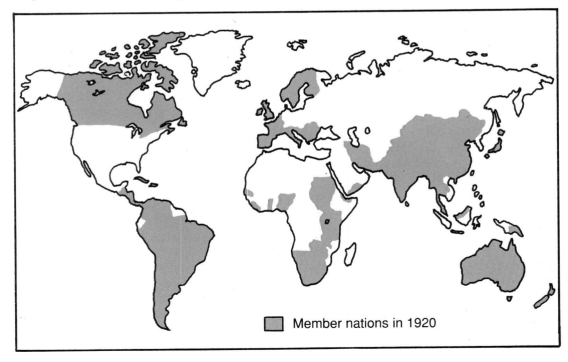

Member nations in 1920

WORK SECTION

Use sources 6.7–8 to help you answer the following questions:

1. Where in Switzerland was the headquarters of the League of Nations?
2. Was Switzerland's offer to give a home to the League's H.Q. accepted because Switzerland was small, neutral, European or mountainous? Choose the one correct answer.
3. Which three important nations were not members of the League in 1920? (Look at the unshaded areas on the map.)
4. Which two of these three important nations joined the League later?
5. a) Which of the following were member-nations of the League in 1920: China, Canada, Germany, Australia, India, Argentina?
   b) Which three were British Empire Nations?

Attempts to keep the Peace

One duty of the League of Nations was to look after the security of the world. This meant keeping all the world's nations at peace. When a nation is attacked by another we say its security is threatened. It no longer feels safe.

What could the League do?

The Problem

The Problem: Nation ⊠ attacks Nation ⊠

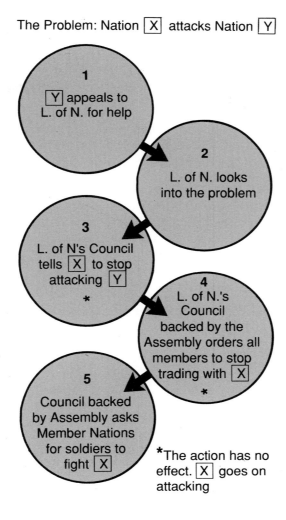

1. ⊠ appeals to L. of N. for help

2. L. of N. looks into the problem

3. L. of N's Council tells ⊠ to stop attacking ⊠ *

4. L. of N.'s Council backed by the Assembly orders all members to stop trading with ⊠ *

5. Council backed by Assembly asks Member Nations for soldiers to fight ⊠

*The action has no effect. ⊠ goes on attacking

The actions taken by the League in Stages 4 and 5 were a way of punishing Nation X. The two types of punishment were called *sanctions*.

The sanctions would only work if all the member-nations co-operated.

When they did there was *international co-operation* and peace had a chance.

Sadly, as you know, not all the world's nations were members of the League. Also there were times when it was very hard to get the member-nations to co-operate. You can now see that the League of Nations had a very difficult job to do!

Attempts to Improve the World

Another duty of the League of Nations was to make the world a better place to live in. In this it was easier to get the member-nations to co-operate. International co-operation seemed the sensible way to deal with many of the world's problems. Here are some of the League's successes:

The settlement of war prisoners and refugees
After the War was over huge numbers of prisoners of war were waiting to be released. The League helped with medical supplies and money. It soon got the prisoners released and returned to Germany.

There were also many people made homeless by the War who wandered about or lived in camps. They were called *refugees*. Again the League gave help by giving food and medical supplies to refugee camps.

The man who led this work for refugees was a Norwegian explorer called Nansen. He gave refugees a special *passport*. It gave them the right to travel freely to look for work. His agents organised transport for refugees to return to their own country. They also helped the refugees find their relatives.

Improvement of conditions for workers

The International Labour Organisation of the League (I.L.O.) printed many reports about workers' conditions in many different countries. The spotlight was put on hours, wages, factory conditions, holidays, safety and so on. If a nation was treating its workers unfairly, the I.L.O. tried to improve conditions by showing how other nations did things better. This is called 'teaching by example'. The I.L.O. had two big successes:

1 All member nations agreed to ban the employment of children.

2 All member nations agreed to ban the use of white lead, which is poisonous, in paint.

Fighting against slavery

The League set up a Department of Slavery. It sent out enquires to all member-nations to find out where slavery still existed. It hoped that member-nations would co-operate to bring trading in slaves to an end. But as late as 1937 the problem of slavery still existed.

Campaign to improve health

The League organised international co-operation to bring about a big improvement in world health. League reports gave evidence to governments about trading in illegal drugs. It warned member-nations about the danger of using these drugs. It tried to stop the drug trade. But it had little success.

One of the worst diseases spreading at this time was leprosy. The League gave help to nations with lepers. It also gave money to doctors who were fighting against leprosy.

Source 6.10 _____

A Reply from the Government of the Sudan to the League's Enquiry about Slavery:

Governor General's Office
Khartoum, 12 April 1927

To the Secretary-General
The League of Nations

In the provinces north of Khartoum the number of slaves still living with their masters has become very small, chiefly as the result of the publicity given to the possibilities of freedom and the increased opportunities for free employment offered by various Government and private firms.

In the extreme south slavery may be said to be non-existent as no slave-owning communities exist there.**"**

Source 6.9 _____

A Nansen Passport

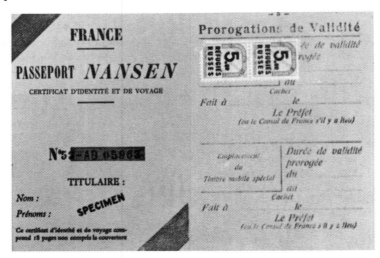

From the League of Nations Handbook, 1923:

❝ The International Labour Organisation was set up on 11 April 1919 as Part XIII of the Treaty of Versailles.

Purposes:

To contribute to the creation of lasting peace by increasing *social justice*.

To improve, through international action, labour conditions and living standards. ❞

WORK SECTION

Use sources 6.9–11 to help you answer the following questions:

1 The special Nansen Passport was used by refugees to:
get free transport
find accommodation
travel freely to look for work
help them find their relations
Copy the correct ending to the sentence.

2 Five of the statements below are ways by which the League tried to improve the world. Choose the five correct statements from the list below:
a) Fighting against slavery
b) Stopping the trade in alcohol
c) Fighting against cruelty to animals
d) Stopping the trade in drugs
e) Giving help to lepers
f) Stopping the employment of children
g) Improving conditions of workers
h) Pulling down slums and badly built houses

i) Improving the lighting of streets

3 Why did the I.L.O. section of the League of Nations want to increase 'social justice' (source 6.11)? Was it:
a) Because it would make poor nations much richer?
b) Because it would make rich nations much poorer?
c) Because it would help to make peace last a long time?
d) Because it would help to prevent strikes in factories?

Write down the correct answer.

Weakness of the League

Look at the German cartoon in source 6.12. It shows the main reason why the League of Nations was too weak to do its job properly. The League didn't have enough power to stop quarrels and wars and so make the world secure. It had no army and no police force. It could only fire shells made of paper!

But there were other reasons why the League was weak. A club for the whole world could only work properly if the most important nations were members. As you already know, the greatest power in the world, the U.S.A., never joined the League.

Two other great powers weren't members until the League had got going – Germany and Russia. Russia didn't join until 1934. Germany joined in 1926 and then left in 1933.

The two most important nations were Britain and France. They couldn't always agree with each other about what the League should do. These disagreements divided and weakened the League. It got weaker and weaker and was unable to stop the outbreak of the Second World War.

TALKING POINT

Why was the League of Nations too weak to do its job properly? How could it have been made more effective?

Source 6.12 _____

A German cartoon (adapted)

WORD-FILE

Civil Service The organisation of paid officials which helps the government of a country carry out its orders. Its members are civil servants.

Congress The Parliament of the United States of America. It is divided into two parts, the House of Representatives and the Senate.

International Co-operation Friendly help between two nations or several nations. Usually the nations all want to get the same results.

Passport A booklet issued by a government which allows a person to travel freely out of, and back into, a country. It makes clear the owner's identity and the country to which he/she belongs.

Refugee A homeless person who has fled from his/her own country for some reason.

Sanction A penalty or punishment for doing something wrong.

Security A feeling of safety from wars, invasion and other threats. World security is achieved when nations are at peace and don't feel threatened by war.

Social Justice The right of people to a fair deal in life.

President Wilson and the League of Nations

This Extension will look at some of the arguments which President Wilson used to get Americans to accept the Treaty of Versailles. He made many speeches like the one in source 6.13 in many parts of the U.S.A. His arguments won some supporters but they didn't convince the Congress. So Wilson lost his last great battle. America refused to support the Treaty of Versailles and refused to join the League of Nations.

Source 6.13

Extract from President Wilson's Speech at Pueblo, U.S.A. in 1919:

❝ What of our promises to the men that lie dead in France? We said that they went over there not to prove that America had great power or that she was ready for another war, but to see to it that there never was such a war again...

These men were crusaders. They were not going out to prove the power of the U.S.A. They were going out to prove the power of justice and right... Their achievement has made all the world believe in America as it believes in no other nation. There seems to me to stand between us and the rejection of this Treaty the ranks of those boys in khaki...

France was free and the world was free because America had come!

We must not go back on those boys but see the thing through, see it through to the end. The salvation of the world depends upon this decision.❞

Source 6.14

Punch cartoon

OVERWEIGHTED.

PRESIDENT WILSON. "HERE'S YOUR OLIVE BRANCH. NOW GET BUSY."
DOVE OF PEACE. "OF COURSE I WANT TO PLEASE EVERYBODY; BUT ISN'T THIS A BIT THICK?"

ASSIGNMENTS

Use the source information and reference books where necessary to answer the following questions:

1. What does Wilson mean by calling the American soldiers of the First World War, crusaders?
2. In your own words describe what their crusade was about and what President Wilson thought it had achieved.
3. Why would the American 'rejection of this Treaty' mean that Americans would reject the League of Nations?
4. 'France was free and the world was free because America had come!' Explain how far this claim by Wilson is an exaggeration.
5. Look at the cartoon in source 6.14. Explain what President Wilson had done and why the dove of peace was complaining.

Extension 2

The Rules of the League of Nations

The rules for the working of the League were listed in a document called the Covenant of the League of Nations.

This Extension will look at some of these rules. You will see how the rules were designed to help the League bring about international peace and security.

Source 6.15

Extracts from the Covenant of the League of Nations:

❝ • The action of the League under this Covenant shall be brought about through an Assembly and a Council with a permanent Secretariat [paid officials].
• The Assembly shall consist of Representatives of the Members of the League. At meetings, each Member of the League shall have one vote.
• The Council shall consist of Representatives of the chief allied powers, together with Representatives of four other members of the League to be selected by the Assembly from time to time as it thinks fit. At meetings each member of the League on the Council shall have one vote.
• The keeping of peace requires the reduction of national armaments to the lowest point consistent with national safety.
• Any war or threat of war is a matter of concern to the whole League and the League shall take action to safeguard the peace of nations.
• It is to be the friendly right of each member to bring to the attention of the Assembly or Council any matter which threatens international peace.
• The members of the League agree that if there should arise between them a dispute likely to lead to a quarrel, they will submit the matter to the Council and agree in no case to go to war until three months after the Council's judgement.
• Should any member go to war in disregard of the Council's judgement, it shall be regarded to have gone to war against all other members. The League shall cut off trading and recommend what effective military, naval or air force should be used. **❞**

▰▰▰ ASSIGNMENTS ▰▰▰

Use the source information and reference books where necessary to help you answer these questions:
1. How might the League get to know of any dispute between its members which could threaten peace?
2. If members were in dispute with each other what two steps would the League expect these members to take?
3. If such a dispute led to a quarrel and then to war what two actions would the League take?
4. Does the Covenant of the League:
   a) provide machinery to prevent wars from breaking out?
   b) make wars between its members illegal?
   Give reasons for your answer.
5. Why would the non-membership of the U.S.A. make it hard for the League to enforce its actions against any of its members at war?
6. How do the rules of the League of Nations give more weight to the Great Powers although both the Assembly and the Council Members of the League all have one vote each?

7 International Co-operation

Nations in 1920

You will remember that before the War there were six European nations which were Great Powers. They were Britain, France, Italy, Germany, Austria-Hungary and Russia. After the War Austria-Hungary had been split up and would never again be a Great Power.

All the others remained Great Powers but only Britain and France still had enough power to boss other nations around. They had won the War and still had great empires overseas.

Russia had become a Communist nation and had turned her back on the rest of the world.

WHAT YOU WILL LEARN

Unit 7 will help you to understand:

1 That *international co-operation* in the 1920s was intended to bring security and lasting peace.
2 How Germany supported international co-operation, even though she had been defeated.
3 How the problem caused by *reparations* was solved.
4 How some international agreements helped the nations which signed them to find security.
5 The steps taken towards the *disarmament* of the Great Powers.

Italy had hoped to gain some of Germany's Empire in Africa. But she failed and felt she had lost her place among the Great Powers.

Germany had lost the War and her Empire overseas. But she could still be looked upon as a Great Power.

Germany in 1920

Look at the map on p. 72 to remind yourself how large Germany was in 1920. Compare her size with the size of other nations in Europe.

Germany had come out of the War without losing very much of her own land. Germany only lost land which was inhabited by people of other nations in addition to the Germans living there.

The Germans had got rid of the Kaiser and made their nation a republic. Now they had a President and a Parliament which was elected by the people. This made Germany a *democracy* like Britain and France.

The new leaders of Germany wanted to play their part with Britain and France to make the world secure from the danger of war. In other words Germany wanted to co-operate with the other nations. This international co-operation would lead to security and a lasting peace.

But many Germans didn't agree with their leaders. They didn't want Germany to co-operate with Britain and France. They hated the Allies for beating them in the War and also because they were being punished by the Allies after the War.

Many Germans thought that the worst punishment given by the Treaty of Versailles was having to pay reparations to the Allies. These were payments in cash and goods and were fixed at the huge sum of £6600 million.

Germany Couldn't Pay, Wouldn't Pay

This money was meant to pay for all the damage caused by Germany in the War. But the German people hadn't started the War. Why should they have to pay for the actions of the Kaiser and his Government? They had now got rid of the Kaiser and the new German Government was peace-loving.

In any case Germany couldn't afford to pay. She was in a financial mess. Her factories couldn't fill the shops with goods. Wages were low and prices of goods rose to enormous heights. Soon nobody had any money left in the banks.

So in 1923 Germany told the Allies that the payment of reparations would be stopped.

The Anger of France

Britain was prepared to wait for German payments but France wanted the money and goods right away. Remember that the war damage in France was greater. This meant she was due to get more from Germany than any of the other Allies.

When Germany stopped payments in 1923, France sent troops to occupy the rich area of coal mines and factories in Germany called the Ruhr.

It did not solve the problem of Germany's debt. France got very little goods out of the Ruhr because the Germans refused to carry out any orders the French gave them. The loss of production in the Ruhr made it even more difficult for Germany to pay up.

Source 7.1

British cartoon from *Punch* May 1923 (M. Poincaré was the French Prime Minister. Lord Curzon was the Foreign Secretary in the British Government)

SAUCE FROM THE GOOSE.

THE GERMAN GOOSE. "YOU WANTED AN EGG; WELL, THERE YOU ARE. TAKE IT OR LEAVE IT."

M. POINCARÉ. "CALL THAT AN EGG? I CALL IT AN INSULT!"

LORD CURZON. "I AGREE THAT IT'S ON THE SMALL SIDE; STILL, THE BIRD *HAS* STARTED LAYING."

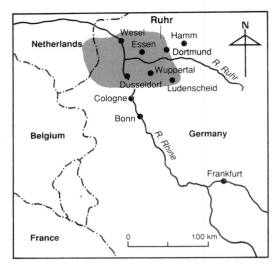

The Ruhr area of Germany

Source 7.2

Speech of Raymond Poincaré:

❝ We are going to look for coal, that's all! If this search gives us the opportunity, sooner or later, of talking with Germany in a more reasonable mood, we will certainly do so. We have no intention of strangling Germany or ruining her. We only want to get from her what we can reasonably expect her to give. ❞

WORK SECTION

Answer the following questions, using sources 7.1–7.4 to help you.

1 Look at the cartoon (source 7.1) which appeared after the French occupied the Ruhr area.
The egg laid by the German goose

J'Y SUIS—J'Y RESTE.

Source 7.3

A British cartoon from *Punch*. The French words mean 'Here I am – Here I stay'

shows that Germany was not giving all that she should to Britain and France. What was Germany supposed to be giving?
2 Why does Poincaré, for France, think this was 'an insult'?
3 How does the cartoonist suggest that:
a) France is the ally taking action against Germany?
b) Britain is the ally taking no action?

Hände weg vom Ruhrgebiet!

Source 7.4

A German poster. The German words mean 'Hands off the Ruhr!'

4 What action did the French take against Germany in 1923 and what did they hope to gain by this action?
5 The cartoon (source 7.3) and the poster (source 7.4) give very different views of the French action against Germany.
a) How does source 7.3 suggest the action could be successful?
b) How does source 7.4 suggest the action will be a failure?

74

c) Which of the two sources gives the more accurate picture of what actually happened?
Give reasons for your answer.

The Dawes Plan

The occupation of the Ruhr by the French threatened the peace and security of Europe. There could never be a lasting peace between France and Germany until the problem of Germany's reparations payments was solved.

In 1924 talks were held between France, Britain and the U.S.A. These talks led to a plan called the Dawes Plan:

* Germany's reparations bill was reduced and she was given more time to pay.

* Germany was loaned a huge sum of money from America to help her develop farms, mines and factories. This would help Germany produce goods with which to pay her debts.

* France agreed to withdraw her troops from the Ruhr.

In this way international co-operation brought about a peaceful solution to a difficult problem.

Gustav Stresemann

In 1923, when Germany was still suffering from the French occupation of the Ruhr, Gustav Stresemann became Germany's Minister of Foreign Affairs.

Stresemann wanted other nations to respect Germany as a Great Power. He wanted to regain the lands she had lost on the eastern frontier. But he also believed that Germany would get nowhere unless she co-operated with other nations. Stresemann wanted international co-operation, peace and security.

This was also what the leaders of France and Britain wanted. They felt they could do business with Stresemann. The prospects for a lasting peace in Europe looked very bright.

German cartoon of Gustav Stresemann

Stresemann's first great success was the Treaty of Locarno. It was considered a great achievement of international co-operation. Gustav Stresemann and Aristide Briand of France were awarded the Nobel Peace Prize for their part in making the agreement.

Stresemann was a great leader. He tried to make Germany more free and *democratic*. He succeeded in building respect for Germany in the rest of the world. But, sadly, he died in October 1929. Men of different views then came to power in Germany.

The Treaty of Locarno, 1925

In October 1925, an international conference was held at Locarno in Switzerland. The leaders of Germany, France, Britain and Italy drew up several agreements designed to bring about security and a lasting peace in Europe:
* The western frontiers of Germany, which had been fixed by the Treaty of Versailles, were accepted by Germany. Therefore Germany wouldn't ever claim Alsace-Lorraine again.
* Germany and France promised never to fight each other again. All arguments between them were to be referred to the League of Nations.
* Britain and Italy agreed to see that France and Germany kept their promises.
* France agreed to help Belgium, Poland and Czechoslovakia, if Germany attacked them.

Germany and the League of Nations

In 1926 Stresemann continued along the path of international co-operation by applying for Germany to join the League of Nations. The application was accepted and Germany was given a seat on the Council of the League beside the other Great Powers.

The Kellogg-Briand Pact, 1928

Aristide Briand was the French Minister of Foreign Affairs. He came forward with a plan that France and the U.S.A. should sign a *pact* to give up war.

Russian cartoon of Aristide Briand

The American Secretary of State, Frank Kellogg, agreed. He felt that other nations should also be invited to sign.

In 1928 the Kellogg-Briand Pact was signed by 65 nations. All of them, led by the U.S.A. and France, agreed to give up war as a way of solving arguments between them.

The Kellogg-Briand Pact was a good example of international co-operation. But it didn't really improve security or ensure a lasting peace in the world. There was no way of punishing any nation in the Pact that decided to break the agreement. The Pact allowed its members to fight in self-defence if they were attacked. What was to stop a nation pretending it had been attacked and then start a war?

Real security in the world could only be got by disarmament. This would mean an international agreement to get rid of armies, navies and air forces and their weapons of war.

Source 7.5

Winds of Change 1914–1939 **by Harold Macmillan:**

❝ The Locarno Treaty seemed a real landmark in the search for peace. The meeting in London, where Austen Chamberlain* welcomed Briand, Stresemann and other statesmen, was a famous event. Apart from the points agreed, such as the confirmation of Germany's western frontiers, the [later] signing of the Locarno Treaty was a real gain.

Abroad, we felt reasonably secure. The British Foreign Secretary* assured us that the spirit of Locarno would spread over Europe. ❞
* Austen Chamberlain was the British Foreign Secretary

Source 7.6

The Treaty of Locarno 1925 (adapted):

❝ Treaty between Germany, Belgium, France, Great Britain and Italy. These parties confirm the continuation of the present frontiers between Germany and Belgium and between Germany and France as fixed by the Treaty of Versailles of 28 June 1919.

Germany and Belgium, and also Germany and France, agree that they will never attack or invade each other or go to war against each other.

If one of the parties claims that this Treaty has been broken in any way, it shall bring the problem at once before the Council of the League of Nations. ❞

Source 7.7

The Times **28 August 1928:**

❝ The ceremony was impressive although it was short and simple. Those who were present will not easily forget the occasion. The representatives of the greatest powers of the modern world 'faithfully promised' that they condemned going to war for the solution of international arguments.

They also gave up war as an instrument in their relations with each other. ❞

Source 7.8

Frank Kellogg signing the Kellogg-Briand Pact at Versailles on 31 August 1928

WORK SECTION

Answer the following questions, using sources 7.5–7.8 to help you.

1 Which nations did each minister for foreign affairs, mentioned in source 7.5, represent?

2 Explain why Macmillan called the Treaty of Locarno 'a real landmark in the search for peace' (source 7.5). Was it because:
   a) Germany and France agreed to disarm?
   b) Germany and France promised not to fight?
   c) Germany and France promised not to fight each other?
   d) Germany and France agreed to share Alsace-Lorraine?
   Write down the one correct answer using source 7.6.

3 What agreement was made at Locarno about Germany's western frontiers? (source 7.6)

4 Use both source 7.7 and source 7.8 to explain why the Kellogg-Briand Pact was 'most impressive'.

5 Why do you think the Pact turned out to be a great disappointment?

Steps towards Disarmament

People remembered that one of the main causes of the First World War had been the heavy build-up of armies and navies, weapons and warships. This is called *re-armament*. After the War, many people believed that this process should be reversed. Nations should gradually get rid of their armed forces together with their weapons, warships and fighter-planes. This is called disarmament.

Few people thought that disarmament should be total. That would leave a nation with no means of defence at all. Disarmament should go on until each nation had enough arms for its own defence – and no more. Disarmament would give security by making war less likely to break out. It was the road to a lasting peace.

There were two big steps forward towards disarmament in the 1920s:

1st Step – The Disarmament of Germany.

You will remember that by the Treaty of Versailles Germany had to get rid of her air force, tanks and submarines and could only have a small army and navy. The Great Powers forced Germany to do what the Treaty of Versailles said. They made sure that Germany's army and navy would not be large enough to start another war.

2nd Step – Treaty of Washington 1921.
After the War Japan began to build up her navy. She was the strongest nation in the Pacific Ocean and so didn't need a huge navy for defence. The U.S.A. and Britain believed that Japan was threatening the security of China.

What should they do about it? At first they agreed to build up the American and British navies. By this they hoped to make Japan too frightened to start a war. Then they decided to try to prevent war through international co-operation. In 1921 the Americans organised a conference in Washington, capital of the U.S.A. The Treaty of Washington was signed. By this Treaty, the U.S.A., Britain and Japan all agreed that disarmament was the way to prevent war. They all agreed to reduce the size of their navies.

Ten Years of Hope

In this Unit you have looked at many examples of international co-operation. This made the ten years from 1920 to 1930 years of real hope. People really believed that a lasting peace could be built on the foundations of trust and friendship between nations.

But this quickly became an impossible dream. In the 1930s the Allies couldn't make Germany stick to the rules fixed by the Treaty of Versailles. The Germans refused to remain the only Great Power in a state of disarmament. The re-armament of the new Germany, led by Adolf Hitler,

caused the nations to face the agony of the Second World War.

WORD-FILE

Democracy A nation which chooses or elects its government is called a democracy. The nation also elects representatives to sit in an assembly or parliament. The government must get the agreement of parliament to pass its laws.

Democratic Anything which is like a democracy. You are democratic if you believe in freedom and want to have a say in how your nation is governed.

Disarmament Getting rid of or reducing the weapons, warships and fighter planes of a nation and reducing its armed forces.

International Co-operation Nations working together to bring about something they all want in common.

Pact Another word for a treaty or agreement made between nations.

Re-armament The opposite to disarmament. A building up of weapons, etc. and of the armed forces of a nation.

Reparations Money and other kinds of payment made as compensation for war damage caused by a defeated nation.

TALKING POINT

Which was the more likely to make a lasting peace after the First World War – the disarmament of Germany alone or the disarmament of all the Great Powers?

Extension 1

German Resistance in the Ruhr

This Extension will focus on the attitude of the German Government and people to the occupation of the Ruhr area by the French from 1923 to 1925.

Source 7.9

German Government Order, January 1923:

❝The action of the French Government in the Ruhr area is a serious breaking of international law and of the Treaty of Versailles.

As a consequence all orders directed to German officials [by the French] in the course of this action are unlawful. The German Government therefore orders all its officials not to obey the instructions of the occupying forces.❞

ASSIGNMENTS

Use the source information and reference books where necessary.

1 Explain why the Germans were right to claim that by occupying the Ruhr area the French had broken:
   a) International law
   b) the Treaty of Versailles (source 7.10).
2 What were the German officials in the Ruhr instructed to do by the German Government? (source 7.9)
3 What evidence does source 7.10 give to show that the French occupation caused hardships for the Germans?
4 What reasons did the German Government give for calling off its order of January 1923 instructing officials to disobey the French? (source 7.10)
5 What problem had led to the French occupation of the Ruhr area?
6 How was that problem eventually solved?

Source 7.10

German Government Proclamation, September 1923:

❝ On 11 January French troops occupied the German Ruhr area. Since then over 180 000 German men, women, old people and children have been driven from house and home. Millions of Germans no longer know what personal freedom is. Countless acts of violence have happened during the occupation, more than one hundred fellow Germans have lost their lives, and hundreds are still shut up in prison.

There was a resistance against the unlawful nature of the invasion. The population refused to work under foreign bayonets.

The Government undertook to do what it could for our suffering fellow Germans. In the past week support reached 3500 billion marks. *Economic life in Germany is disrupted. If we go on with our present resistance it will be impossible to secure a bare existence for our people.

To save the life of the people and the Nation we face today the bitter necessity of calling off the struggle. **❞**
* German money

Extension 2

Gustav Stresemann, Minister of Foreign Affairs

In the letter below Stresemann explains his views on Germany's relations with other nations.

Source 7.11

Letter of Gustav Stresemann to ex-Prince William, Sept 1925:

❝ There are three great tasks that face us in the immediate future –

In the first place the solution of the reparations question in an acceptable way for Germany. Also the assurance of peace, which is essential for the recovery of our strength.

Secondly, the protection of Germans abroad who now live under foreign domination in foreign lands.

The third great task is the re-adjustment of our eastern frontiers.

If we want to secure our aims we must concentrate on these tasks.

The Security Pact ensures peace for us and makes Britain a protector of our western frontiers. The Pact also rules out any military conflict with France for the recovery of Alsace-Lorraine. . .

It is my belief that we are not choosing to support either the east [Russia] or the west [Britain and France] by joining the League of Nations. **❞**

▩▩▩▩ ASSIGNMENTS ▩▩▩▩

Use the source information and reference books where necessary.
1 What would the Germans regard as 'an acceptable way' of solving the reparations question?
2 Give one example of where, since 1919, Germans were living abroad under 'foreign domination'.
3 Why did Stresemann want the 're-adjustment of our eastern frontiers'?
4 What was 'the Security Pact'?
5 Explain the importance of this Pact for Germany.
6 In what ways was Gustav Stresemann a good and successful foreign minister for Germany?

Index